ENDORSEMENTS

A pleasure to read yet substantial in its depth! Dr. Remilyn Mueller is a voice that is both encouraging and provoking, turning the age-old academic advice into something valuable and applicable for the AI and Technology 2.0 era. This book weaves faith-rooted wisdom with touching and funny anecdotes that pulse with spiritual resilience amidst the burnout era of adult education.

Dr. Gerzon Tuazon, Senior Lecturer at Eastern Institute of Technology, New Zealand

As someone who has spent years teaching nontraditional and adult learners at both two-year and four-year colleges, "You're Not Alone!" struck me as an extraordinary resource—one that truly understands the lived experience of the adult student. Dr. Mueller speaks not only from academic expertise but also from personal struggle, spiritual grounding, and a genuine heart for learners pursuing education in the middle of real life.

Her words echo what I've seen time and again in my own students: Doubt, overwhelm, and the recurring question, "Did I make a mistake?" This book offers a resounding "no"—reminding readers that persistence, faith, and practical strategies can carry them through. Dr. Mueller's voice is both instructional and pastoral, providing gentle yet powerful truth and hope for anyone who feels stuck, stretched thin, or scared to begin. It's a must-read for every adult learner and every educator who supports them.

Stephanie Miller, M.A., Writing & Spiritual Growth Coach

You're Not Alone is a lifeline for any online student who has ever felt isolated, bewildered, or overwhelmed on their academic journey. It is a treasure trove of wisdom drawn from real-life hurdles and triumphs that speak deeply to your heart by weaving in the undeniable truth of God's Word. More than just a guide, it is a transformative reminder of God's promises, promises that you can firmly anchor in, enabling you to flourish in the purpose He has set for you.

Dr Jhona Gamez, Faculty Chair at
MAPUA-Malayan Colleges Laguna, Philippines

The book that Dr. Mueller wrote is a testament that the journey is more important than the destination. Every person you meet along the way will help you shape what you will become as an individual who is going through many struggles in life. This book will help you manage your life's expectations through the grace of God. This is a good read for all of us who are battling our challenges.

Dr. Pamela Joyce M. Eleazar,
University of the Philippines, Los Baños

Reading this book felt like sitting down with a trusted friend. Dr. Remilyn Mueller's words are down-to-earth, heartfelt, and genuinely encouraging. I found myself wishing I had this book beside me throughout my dissertation journey. It offers not just practical strategies, but emotional and spiritual support that speaks directly to the online adult learner's experience. It's an easy yet powerful read, blending personal reflection with actionable advice. This book is a must-have for any learner seeking motivation, faith, and a reminder that they're truly not alone."

Dr. Sarah Robertson,
Associate Professor at Grand Canyon University, USA

As a Success Coach for online college students, I absolutely see the intentional and authentic value of Remilyn's book. It isn't just because it is a neatly put-together book of experience and wisdom, but every bit of prayer and heart that has gone into this reading is GOLDEN! Remilyn writes with clear and compelling effort that will be your most faithful and treasured guide as you journey to your FINISH line and the prize of earning your degree.

Julie Kenzler, Author and Success
Coach at Arizona State University, USA

DEDICATION

To

The two fathers I know.

My first-grade teacher, my dad,

Eladio

whose passion for reading books impacted my love for learning.

and

My father-in-law,

Brian

whose life's work and leadership opened my eyes to the many
possibilities in higher education.

ACKNOWLEDGMENTS

To my husband, Johnny, thank you so much for your love, understanding, and full support in this writing project. I felt cared for when you accompanied me to my writing conferences, did all the driving, and made sure I had my daily dose of coffee and desserts. All these expressions of love allowed me to focus on learning about the world of publishing instead of worrying about navigating strange places on my own. When we're at home, thank you for giving me space and time to write. You understand when I have to close the door of my office, or play jazz music on TV in the living area as I occupy the couch for my cozy writing space, and you retreat to the other room to watch your sports or news. You also nodded with understanding at the many times I needed to leave the house and go to the coffee shop to focus on the final revisions.

To my siblings: Eli, Rachel, Regina, and Ebenezer, thank you for your continued support and encouragement in all my endeavors, including this writing project. Special thanks to Regina for providing insights on the early draft of this book. I had to weed out some of the details you pointed out as irrelevant or unclear to the readers. I also thank Ebenezer for helping me with the branding, website development, and other technical layers involved in book publishing.

To my mom, Remedios, and my mother-in-law, Paula, thank you for your unceasing prayers, your concerns, and your questions about this project. This book is dedicated to the two fathers I know who inspired me to write, but it was the prayers of these two mothers that sustained me to finish it.

To my developmental editor, Abby McDonald, thank you for your patience when I could not meet deadlines. Your sharp eyes scrutinized the manuscript from its early development stages to its final copy. From grammatical and mechanical errors to logical organization of content, you made sure that everything makes sense to the readers.

To friends, colleagues, and strangers who signed up as beta readers or as members of the launch team, thank you so much! This book would not be in this shape and form if not for your valuable feedback. Special thanks to Dr. Jeff Cranmore for writing the foreword and to Stephanie Miller, Julie Kenzler, Dr. Jhona Gamez, Dr. Sarah Robertson, Dr. Pamela Joyce Eleazar, and Dr. Gerzon Tuazon for reviewing this book in its entirety. Your insights and perspectives polished the finishing touches of this book, and I am confident to release it after it passed your scrutiny. To Ms. Vilma Michaud, thank you for always reminding me that you and your whole team of prayer warriors are praying for me. You uplifted me when I was struggling for breakthroughs in the final revisions of the manuscript.

To the rest of my friends who patiently listened as I shared my writing updates. You did not give up believing that I could do it, and you kept encouraging and praying for me. Thanks to our Christ's Church of the Valley (CCV) small group who always pray for me: Mark, Heather, Rachel, and the rest. To all my lady friends who were excited for me to get done: Juvy, Tami, Angie, Maria, Alice, Lorna, Becky, Misty, Fatima, Donna, and Bree. Just knowing that they look forward to having this book in their hands, even though they are not my ideal audience, always pushes me to keep writing.

To all my author and entrepreneur friends that I met for the last two years since I started this writing journey, thank you for leading the way. I am so blessed to know you, watch you get published, and start or expand your businesses. Special thanks to Kristen, who coached me when I was struggling to finish the revisions. Thank you, Lisa, Brad, Kimberly, Heather, Amy, and Justin for leading the way, always willing to help by answering my questions.

To the countless people in my life who in one way or another have inspired me to write this book. To all my students, and my colleagues, past and present: You have taught me a lot more than you would ever know. Your lives are living testament of God's love and sustaining grace.

To God Almighty, the waymaker, the promise-keeper, and the light in my darkness. Thank you for loving and sustaining me. I know You will bring Your work in me to completion. All glory, honor, and praise belongs to you!

TABLE OF CONTENTS

FOREWORD

Dr. Jeff Cranmore

Dissertation Chair at Grand Canyon University

When Dr. Mueller asked me to read this manuscript, of course I jumped at the chance. I had worked with her as her chair throughout the dissertation process, but hearing her journey from her perspective was eye-opening. Dr. Mueller brings to life the journey of online learning, from the perspective of a teacher and student, while engaging readers through stories. This in itself is worth the read, but the way she is able to incorporate her faith feels like she is speaking directly to the reader. Or more appropriately, she has found the perfect examples from Scripture to speak directly to the reader.

Being an online learner can feel lonely, and sometimes you feel like you are on your own. Dr. Mueller captures this journey in a way that is honest and relatable and is the perfect motivator for those in the middle of the work. The stories she shares from her own experience and those of her students and fellow classmates capture the essence of the journey, and remind us of our "why?" Why did we choose this? Why are we putting ourselves through this? Once we are able to have that question answered, we must find a way to remember that answer and refer to it as we face all of the obstacles.

Finally, Dr. Mueller offers sage advice for all of those in the process, from setting schedules, to support systems, to how to break down tasks into manageable chunks. Beyond that, she provides valuable insight into the technology issues, taking full advantage of resources–both financial and support at the university. And of course, she outlines what to do once the degree is completed, and how to set yourself up for success in the job market, in both private and academic settings. Whether you are in the process yourself, know someone who is in the middle of a degree, or even considering starting a new degree, Remilynn Mueller clearly reminds us all, "You're Not Alone!"

PREFACE

I know you already have a lot of readings. A lot of deadlines. And you are juggling a lot of things in your life. You have a family to care for, a full-time job, bills to pay, a community to serve, relationships to nourish, social events to attend, and so much more.

So, I am grateful that you picked this book and took an interest in reading it. I hope you will devour the message on every page and finish reading with a hope-filled heart, inspired in your pursuit of higher education with eyes on the prize as you run towards the finish line. That finish line is on the stage when you march on your graduation day to receive your diploma.

Thank you for giving me time as I speak from my heart to yours. The message in this book is an overflow from my years of being a student as I pursued my bachelor's, master's, and doctoral degrees. This is also my thanksgiving offering from two decades of combined teaching at different levels from kindergarten, elementary, high school, college students, and now doctoral learners. Most importantly, may the power of the Holy Spirit speak in your heart and life as you taste God's word embedded in the stories and pages of this book.

Nonetheless, my inspiration for writing this book came from the two fathers I know. First, my dad, who was my first-grade teacher. His life exemplifies lifelong learning and a passion for teaching others. Secondly, my father-in-law, whose life's work and leadership are testified through the exponential growth of one of the largest Christian universities in America. His wisdom and leadership pioneered the development of many online programs, making online education accessible and affordable for many learners across the country and beyond. His positive influence impacted thousands of employees and graduates in both the traditional campus and online programs. Above all, he embodies servant leadership in his daily life. One of the earliest memories I have of him was when the whole family was eating at a restaurant. Somebody spilled water, and he was the first to stand up and get a rag from the kitchen and wipe it dry. He did not tell one of his sons, nor call one of the restaurant crew to do it; he did the job himself. He is a man of accomplishments and high position, but at that moment, he taught me a lesson about servant leadership.

The message in this book burned incessantly in my heart long before my fingers were able to type it out in written form. I want to walk with you as you navigate this academic journey, and accompany you in your isolation and desperation as you try to figure out how you can flourish and enjoy this adventure you have thrown yourself into. One of my greatest desires for you, as an online learner, is to flourish in your academic journey by relying on the promises of God's Word. It is my prayer that you will no longer dread opening your student portal and breathe a sigh of despair saying, "Not another deadline!" whenever you see that another task or assignment is due and you have not yet recuperated from the brunt of the previous submissions.

It is my prayer that you will not take your physical and mental health for granted, or sacrifice your relationships at the altar of academic pursuits. I pray that as you read this book, you will realize that you do not have to wait until you graduate to flourish. That right now, you can seek meaning and purpose to what you are doing, that your character and virtues are aligned to that which you labor for, and that you will surround yourself with good relationships that bring happiness and life satisfaction in this mighty conquest. I hope that you will find the practical nuggets of wisdom from this book helpful as you fight for your dream of getting a degree.

Interwoven in this book are my personal stories and anecdotes. I shared what led me to online education and how it paved the way for me to get my master's and doctoral degrees. My dissertation was about flourishing, and I have learned a lot from reading relevant literature about the topic of human flourishing. Reading journal articles may seem like a daunting task, but I learned how to enjoy it. One day, as I was reading journal articles for my dissertation, a thought crossed my mind that the wisdom from these wonderful research papers must be shared in a book without the distractions of in-text citations. That was when the idea to write a book was born: Not an academic book, but a book related to academics with the wisdom and inspiration from God's Word and research papers combined.

Aside from my personal experiences as a student, I have drawn wisdom and inspiration from my online adult learners. All names referring to students are fictitious and their collective stories are presented as a singular person. For example, the story of Gina in Chapter 1 is a story of many students. My students' quest for an academic degree is unstoppable and admirable. When I encounter students facing similar situations, problems, or struggles, the first thing that comes to my mind is, *"You're not alone!"* Online education can be isolating and this book is to let you know that you are not alone in this academic journey.

The Word of God is filled with promises, inspiration, and wisdom where you can draw strength and hope from. As you read through the chapters, stop and meditate on the Bible verses that I quote. Claim them as your own message from God. Write them on Post-it notes and place them on your computer. Pray with some of these verses before you begin doing an assignment.

This book is my academic life's work, turned into a creative form for you to enjoy and learn from. This is the culmination of my personal stories, my own educational journey, the influence of those I dearly loved, and the impacts of my mentors. Intricately woven in these pages are the promises of God's Word that held me through the years. I am passing these on to you. You're not alone in your dreams and struggles in this academic journey. Make this book your friend and company until you cross that stage on your graduation day.

Visualize. Choose. Overcome. Thrive.

You're not alone! May this four-part book teach you how you can flourish as an online learner with faith and success strategies.

Blessings,
Dr. Mueller

Part 1

VISUALIZE

Focus: Grounding Your Identity and Faith Before Growth

"Where there is no vision, the people perish...," Proverbs 29:18, (KJV)

I don't know how to paint, and due to past failures at any attempt, I had no interest in pursuing it until somebody introduced a paint-by-number kit to me. A paint-by-number kit has a picture with lots of little spaces and each space has a number. There is also a set of paints and each color has a matching number to the one on the picture. You will then paint each space with the right color. All these colors will come together to make a beautiful painting like magic; it's almost like a puzzle but done with paint. The beautiful outcome can easily deceive an untrained eye. However, a close inspection will reveal the faint lines of pre-drawn numbered spaces that guided the *painter.*

Most of the time, it will be hard for you to see the picture on the black and white numbered spaces drawn on the canvas until the colors of the paint pop out. So, what you do is open one color of paint, let's say, #1. Then, you look for all the spaces with the number "1" marked on it. You paint each tiny piece with that color, then you move on to the next number and corresponding color. A space can be big, or tiny as a dot. The number of colors varies from 10-30 depending on how complex the painting is. A difficult section will only start making sense as a picture starts to emerge. There may be sections that are abstract and it is hard to guess what they are for. For example, a really tiny speck of a circle, like a dot, that you need to paint with black does not make sense. Only after you complete the painting will it make sense when you see that in the big picture, it is the eye of a frog.

Your degree is the big picture. However, embedded in getting your degree is a list of courses and other requirements. Within each course are tasks, sometimes it's a big assignment, and sometimes it is simple and easy such as a little response participating in a discussion. Imagine these as the spaces on the paint-by-number picture. When you are currently struggling with a difficult "space," such as an assignment, it is hard to see the part it plays in the big picture. Some students may get stuck in one "space" and in their frustration wonder about its relevance to their dream job after getting the degree. As a professor, I teach introductory courses that prepare freshmen for their program. Whether they are at the undergraduate or doctoral level, there are times when students come in with an attitude that the course I teach has no value for them. They leave hurtful comments such as, "I just want to become a teacher. I don't see what this assignment about time management, or this requirement to meet the word count in the discussion forum, has anything to do with my dreams!" Months or years later, some would come back to me and say thank you because what they learned in my course finally made sense!

Close your eyes for a moment, and in your head, visualize your big picture. Your big picture can be yourself walking across the graduation stage to the music of the graduation march. You are shaking hands with the university administrators, one of them hands you your diploma, and then you turn to face the audience with a glowing face as a photographer points a camera to immortalize and capture the moment in a picture. Perhaps a tear or two blurs your vision as you beam, proud of your achievement. Somewhere in the audience, your family is clapping and screaming your name wildly as you exit the stage. It only takes about fifteen seconds, but it was a walk you will never forget.

Or perhaps, your big picture is that you see yourself having your own office, finally promoted as a manager. You have a large clean desk, matched with a comfortable swivel chair and a posh carpet. On your desk is your computer, and a nameplate with your position spelled right under your name. Finally, you are the manager! Not only that, but a few weeks later, you receive your paycheck and your eyes cannot believe the pay bump you received. You know great days are ahead as you are now able to provide a better life for yourself and your loved ones.

Big pictures may differ for individual online students. It could be that you are standing in the front of a room of wide-eyed pupils, finally a teacher! It could be that you are at a bedside, administering shots and medications, finally a nurse! It could be that you are headed to New York meeting with investors, finally a business person! Whatever your big picture is, it is important that as you traverse this educational feat, you keep this picture close in your heart and in a clear view. It is better to draw it, or if you can't draw, at least let it out in written form with vivid descriptions. Hang this visual reminder on the wall by your computer, or use it as a screensaver.

When I was pursuing my master's degree, I printed a picture of the special sash called *sablay* [1] and taped it on the graduate folder where I kept my printed materials handy. At one point, I also made it as the cover photo of my social media page. *Sablay* is a highly-regarded academic regalia replacing the common cap and gown, and its design is exclusive for the University of the Philippines. Then, on my doctoral journey, when I was writing my dissertation, I printed a picture of *How to Eat an Elephant* [2] and marked each bite I finished. I have this *elephant* taped right on the wall by my computer desk. These visuals held the vision, my big picture, in clear sight. And when the going gets tough, these pictures remind me that the tough must keep going.

This section delves into that big picture. Read some familiar stories of typical online students and chuckle to yourself as they resonate with yours. Then, take a hard look at your situation. Draw that big picture and remind yourself that you are not alone. You are made for a bigger purpose, and you've got to keep on keeping on.

---

1   The *Sablay* is the official academic costume of the University, replacing upon its introduction in 1990 and its official adoption in 2000, the traditional mortarboard (cap) and toga. https://our.upd.edu.ph/acad.php

2   "How do you eat an elephant?" is answered by "one bite at a time." It is a metaphor for breaking down a large, daunting task into smaller, manageable steps. Here's the sample worksheet https://organizingmaven.com/wp-content/uploads/2015/09/Easy-Goal-Setting-Worksheet.pdf

Chapter 1

STUCK ISN'T
THE END OF THE STORY

"When you pass through the waters, I will be with you; and through the rivers, they shall not overwhelm you; when you walk through fire, you shall not be burned, and the flame shall not consume you." Isaiah 43:2 (ESV)

Gina quietly closed the nursery room door and tiptoed across the hallway.

Her watch read 11:11!

She sighed and went to the kitchen counter, where she left her laptop open. The laptop's battery had died because she'd forgotten to plug it in before her six-month-old baby cried for attention. She was so exhausted that she fell asleep while rocking the fussy baby. Now, she had less than an hour left before midnight, signaling the deadline for an assignment in her online course. A few pages of the journal articles she printed to use as her resources for her assignment were strewn across the kitchen floor, unread. She surveyed the messy kitchen and noted the dishes piled high on the sink, leftover food on the stove, dirty pots and pans, sticky floors, and scattered toys everywhere. She hadn't cleaned the kitchen, nor tidied the whole place since yesterday because she was trying to finish all her weekly assignments first. Unfortunately, this kitchen counter was the only place in the cramped apartment where she could study and work.

Her heart skipped a beat as she remembered she still had much to do to finish her assignment before the clock struck twelve! She grabbed the charger from the drawer and plugged up her laptop. She stared at the clock once more as the computer stirred to life. She needed to focus on finishing this assignment. Her professor had already accepted her late work for the past two weeks without any deductions. But he told her to quit making this a habit, and that he would apply the university policy of 10% deduction if she submitted an assignment late again. She did not want to get deductions, because her performance in this course had been very poor already. With the remaining weeks for this course, it would be a miracle if she could still pull a passing grade. So, she needed to finish this assignment on time!

Her fingers grew sweaty. Her head spun. Her feet suddenly went cold. Her heart beat faster and faster. What was happening? She grabbed the counter for support and breathed for a second. She grabbed a glass of water nearby and gulped, willing her heart to calm down. What was wrong with her? Why was this happening more frequently? Did she have a grave heart condition? Or was it another episode of a panic attack? She knew she could pull this together, but what made her think she could pursue a college degree despite her messy life situation? Then, she wondered, "Did I make a mistake enrolling in college?"

Did I Make a Mistake?

Like Gina, I asked myself this question throughout my academic journey while taking my master's and Ph.D. degrees. Did I make a mistake? What have I gotten myself into? I never doubted my desire for a college degree, and I had a blast from the traditional college campus experience. However, my master's and Ph.D. programs were online, and I had questioned, wondered, cried, screamed, and yelled at myself many times when the nights were dark, hopes were bleak, and I was the only soul awake in the house of peacefully sleeping people.

Why am I doing this?

When will I allow this torture to myself to end?

Is this even God's will for me?

Did I make a mistake in pursuing graduate school?

I have spent countless nights burning the midnight oil, barely beating the red light as my assignments went through the 11:59 PM deadline mark, right before the clock struck midnight and the submission box closed. I was a true to life *Cinderella*!

I thought I was done studying after getting my master's degree. But all the pain and struggles were forgotten and faded away in the background when I crossed the finish line. The euphoria, the uncontainable joy of walking across the stage on my graduation, made me hunger for more. So, on to my doctoral journey! However, the same mental torture took its toll while getting my Ph.D.

Sleepless nights.

Cups of coffee.

Crispy, crunchy snacks to keep my eyes and brain awake.

Endless readings from multiple resources.

Wrist-cramping assignments.

Never-ending, soul-sucking, iterative dissertation process.

And worse, unwanted weight gain in what I call my *dissertation belly*.

The last one is a grim reminder of the sedentary hours I spent sitting down as I was held hostage in the research concentration camp. Most of the time, I was in despair, and at some point during my Ph.D., I experienced anxiety and panic attacks, which never happened when I studied in college or took my master's. The episodic attacks of depression, anxiety, and panic attacks would frequent me as I was nowhere near completion of the milestones with fast-approaching deadlines. The younger me would have had a strong, adrenaline rush that worked magic as I beat each deadline. However, during my Ph.D., the opposite happened. I was gripped in fright, helpless as my mind shut down as if my world was collapsing. I couldn't think. I couldn't write. I felt defeated.

But all through these academic journeys, God was there. He showed me that it was not only the destination—the graduation—that matters. It was the journey itself. At some point in my pain, He showed me that He could use it for His purpose and glory. No, the depressive thoughts, the anxiety, and the panic attacks did not disappear like magic. However, God led me to resources that helped me deal with them, lessening their grip and power on me until they completely disappeared. I read books by Christian neurologists, psychologists, and the Bible. God showed and taught me ways to flourish and find joy, not after, but during the process of going through the hurdles in my academic pursuits.

It Is OK Not to Get a Perfect GPA!

Does your heart palpitate every time you open your student portal and see that an assignment has been graded? Have you set the bar too high for yourself and would not accept a grade except for an A? Do you feel crushed and disappointed if there are few points deducted from your assignment? Do you beat yourself up when your grades come back with anything less than perfect? Are you one of those whose goal is to get a perfect 4.0 GPA?

If you wonder how I managed my anxiety and panic attacks, I reflected on what causes them. It was my goal to get a perfect 4.0 GPA! I was too hard on myself. Finally, I came to peace that it was OK not to get a perfect GPA. I set expectations on myself, so high that it was causing panic attacks when I was running out of time to do a "perfect" assignment. Since college on to my master's degree, I have always been the red-light beater. No, not in driving but in the submission of assignments. So when I was doing my Ph.D., to help curb my anxiety, I had to quit being a red light beater. I had a hard time changing this habit. First, I submitted a few hours earlier than the deadline. Then, I made it a day before the deadline. Sometimes, I was able to submit it a few days ahead of the deadline. I looked at the assignments as if they were *enemies* I needed to attack and defeat as soon as the topic week opened. Through these strategies—mindset coupled with actions—my panic attacks disappeared. I ended up with a good GPA. Not perfect, but a Ph.D. is still a Ph.D. perfect GPA or not.

So, no. I did not make a mistake in any of my decisions to pursue all these degrees.

And neither have you.

You Should Flourish *Now*!

God reminded me that as His child, I do not have to wait until graduation to flourish. He made known to me the path of life. There can be fullness of joy and pleasure even in the midst of academic woes. How? In His presence. At His right hand.

Yes, there were still moments of beating the red light of tight deadlines. Yes, there were still episodes of anxiety and panic attacks especially during the dissertation stage. But as I learned to trust God for His grace as I do the parts I can and surrender to Him the things I cannot control, the more manageable those moments became. Flourishing became the topic of my dissertation. But who reads dissertations? That's when God gave me the desire to share the knowledge, wisdom, and insights I learned by writing a book–this book! Writing this book became part of that purpose that went beyond the pursuit of a Ph.D.

"You make known to me the path of life; in your presence, there is fullness of joy; at your right hand are pleasures forevermore."
Psalm 16:11 (ESV)

As you traverse your academic journey, you will find yourself sinking in doubt and wondering if you made a mistake in pursuing a degree. At whatever point of your academic journey you are in right now, whether you are just starting, in the middle, or running towards the finish line, I want to encourage you not to give up. There is hope, joy, and opportunities to flourish. Find a purpose behind that pain, and the sacrifice you are making now will all be worth it. God has your back, so you got this!

You Are Not Too Old to Get a College Degree

Maureen is pursuing a business degree in an online program at Grand Canyon University in Arizona, miles away from her South Carolina home. She has already finished seven courses for the past year, and in three more years, if she stays on track with her program plan, she will graduate with a business degree right before she turns 60. Many years ago, at 18, living in a bustling touristy area of downtown Charleston in South Carolina, she did not know what she wanted after high school graduation. She worked as a food server that summer and enjoyed it. She was earning a lot from tips and loved interacting with all types of customers, mostly tourists from all over the country and the world. Working at a restaurant brought her so much satisfaction and joy that she put any college plans on hold. The plan for a gap year was extended into several more years while she worked and cruised a life of parties with friends on boating trips across Carolina waters.

It was on one of these boating trips that she met Tom. A handsome young man who stole her heart. Before she knew it, she was swept off her feet onto a honeymoon and a marriage that lasted for years. Raising six kids required her to stay home while Tom worked to provide for the family. To make ends meet, she tried to sell all kinds of stuff such as lemonade, baked cookies, and handmade jewelry at the old marketplace downtown. She dreamt of having her own jewelry business. Years passed, and the kids had all grown up and left the house. Then, her world fell apart, almost crushing her, when Tom filed for a divorce. All her life was spent taking care of her children and husband. Her identity and worth were interwoven into theirs. So, when the children grew up, and Tom left her, she felt unsure about her purpose in life.

She got a job at a jewelry shop to support herself as she figured out what to do for the rest of her life. One day, a lady customer approached her and asked for jewelry made of amethysts.

"Purple is the color of our university!" she exclaimed as she daintily examined the earrings. "These would match my clothes when I go to basketball games!"

"Are you a student?" Maureen wondered, because she looked older than a college kid.

"Ah, no. I am a professor!" the lady laughed. "What about you? Do you own this beautiful shop?"

"Nooo. I am an employee," Maureen responded absentmindedly, as she was more curious about the university.

Was it only yesterday when she was unsure what she would do in college, so she kept putting it off? Getting a college degree was her unfinished business. And all these years she had been dreaming of having her own business. Slowly, the bits and pieces merged into one clear picture as she stared at the enthusiastic lady sharing information about the university where she taught. What if she pursued a business degree in college? The lady taught online students. Her students were adults who were busy living their lives, pursuing jobs, and raising kids, and yet, they decided to go back to college and pursue a degree online. Oh, and the professor's oldest student was an eighty-one-year-old veteran who was bored, so he decided to go back to school and get a degree just so he could say that he had done it all! The lady professor could probably sense her suppressed desire to return to college.

"I am 55 now," Maureen interjected. "By the time I'm done, I will be 60 years old!"

"But five years from now, you will still be 60 with or without a degree!" The professor left her a business card. "Think about it. This is something you can do for yourself. Let me know if you have more questions. I can connect you to one of our enrollment counselors."

Thus, her academic journey began. Before she knew it, she was enrolled in her first class. Most of the time, she was proud and happy with her accomplishments. For the past year, her input at work dramatically improved. Her boss began trusting her suggestions and implementing her ideas to improve the business's marketing strategies. She felt that, for the first time in a long time, she was doing something for herself that could not be taken away from her. A college degree.

The academic journey would not be easy, though. Maureen's enrollment counselor gently outlined both the bad and good possibilities that could happen. First, she needed to take student loans to subsidize the expenses for the tuition and needed supplies. She needed to take this degree seriously and finish it. Otherwise, she would end up with debts and no degree. She was told that pursuing an online education was equivalent to having a part-time job. She must allocate 15-20 hours weekly to do the required tasks. She had to reset her priorities and manage her time wisely to live a balanced life. This would mean giving up some of her social events or time hanging out with friends. There would be sleepless nights when she had to finish assignments, or challenging moments when she would find it difficult to comprehend the instructions or reading materials. She needed to beat hard deadlines, and some professors were hard graders who would nitpick on minor mistakes, docking off points. Above all, she had to learn the technology used in education today; he was assured that there would be strong support and guidance. However, she needed to put in a great effort to succeed.

The sound possibilities outweighed the challenges, though! She got to meet peers with the same business interests. She learned from professors and got to be mentored in getting her business plan drafted and ready for implementation. There was an excellent possibility of being part of a network for entrepreneurs or collaborations with other experts in the business field. Furthermore, if she could get investors, she could get the business going even before graduation! Ultimately, if she decided later on not to establish her own business, her degree could land her better job opportunities.

So here she is a year later. Maureen can attest that the academic journey was not easy, and the road ahead looks even more challenging. But she knows she is not alone. She connected well with some of her classmates her age and exchanged contact information so they could communicate outside the course portal. In fact, they already arranged to travel together to Arizona to visit the university, and also see the real Grand Canyon next summer. She knows that they have some struggles, too. Some even have it worse than she does. They are part of her inspiration to keep moving until she reaches the finish line. Her graduation.

You Are Not Alone

You are not alone in this academic journey. The programs delivered through an online platform are designed for adults like you. The ship has sailed. Gone were the days when you were a young eighteen-year-old who was excited to experience college on a traditional campus. Not so long ago, it would be embarrassing for older people to attend college together with rowdy young people. For many, it is not only embarrassing, it is also impossible. What with too many responsibilities as a parent raising kids, and having a full-time job. Or what if you are in the military, or your work requires you to travel most of the time? In these situations, it is impossible to be physically present to attend classes on a campus. But not anymore with the opportunities that online education presents.

I remember in college, I had classmates who were in their 30s, and my friends and I would make fun of them, calling them Grandma or Grandpa. Forgive me, I was a naive teenager too, and I am now embarrassed to share that I joined in the fun. I recall how they would come in late, or have bad grades on their assignments, or had no time to join college activities. They struggled to keep up with the younger learners in retaining information without rereading twice or asking for a repeat of the instructions. Looking back, I now understand why it was that way, and if I could see any of those aforementioned classmates again, I would congratulate them and apologize, telling them that instead of making fun of them, I should have been adoring their ambitions and efforts to make those dreams happen.

And here we are many years later. Slowly, online programs emerged. At first, it was hybrid. Back in 2010, in the Philippines, we were required to go on-site to the campus to take the major exams or make a presentation for the course. But this only happened once in a semester, so it was still convenient. Then, online programs evolved and improved. Right now, with available technologies, a lot of programs would no longer require you to show up on campus. Of course, there are programs that require physical presence such as laboratory work in nursing or engineering programs, but that is still better than physically showing up in classes on a daily basis.

Misconceptions and Expectations

If you are like most online students, you have probably started your online education half-blind without knowing there are costs to count in exchange for a higher education degree pursued online. What I mean by *costs* is not just the financial costs, but other collateral you have to hold on the line such as your health, time, relationships, and many more. Many people have the misconception that pursuing degrees online is easier than the classes in traditional classrooms. They think life will not be affected much, and nothing has to change since they will do it online. If you started with this mindset, you are probably wildly disappointed and frustrated right now. Starting with wrong expectations may be why many people cannot finish their degree. When expectations are not met due to misconceptions, then you get stuck in a rut. To be freed, you need to set the right expectations and straighten those misconceptions.

The Hidden Price

The first step in setting the right expectations and straightening those misconceptions is by counting the cost. Chapter 17 has a section discussing more about counting the cost when setting your priorities. Counting the cost is not merely about your financial responsibilities. It includes everything you need to sacrifice while getting your degree. Even if you started on the wrong foot with misconceptions about online education, there is still time to stop and count the cost. This is crucial for you to move forward and have a rewarding experience obtaining a degree in higher education. Comparing the pros and cons of traditional and online programs might help remind you why the online program is the right fit for you.

Attending classes in traditional classrooms requires a lot of movement and physical energy. In traditional classrooms, students have to drive to the campus, find their classroom, and sit in their chairs for hours as they listen to lectures, collaborate in group activities, answer quizzes and exams, or prepare and present projects in front of the class. One course typically requires 4.5 hours of meeting every week. You also have to factor in the time spent getting ready for a class, driving to the campus, finding a parking spot, walking to the building, finding the classroom, waiting for the professor to arrive, and socializing with classmates. Furthermore, there is homework in preparation for the next meeting. Students also have to study at home to prepare for tests or presentations for the class. Approximately, all these would take 15-20 hours a week. Financially, you also have to spend money for gas or transportation, and snacks because studying makes one hungry! Thus, many people think online education is easier because students only need to log in to the course portal and submit assignments. Sounds easy. But by this time, you probably know that this is a false misconception.

Some of the hidden price of online education is carving a time out of your busy schedule to study. More about time management is discussed in Chapter 12. Remember, you need about 15-20 hours a week to study. Finding that 15-20 hours in your already busy schedule means giving up some things such as time scrolling mindlessly on social media, watching movies, going out for dinners, giving up weekends for social activities, and so on. If you cannot make this temporary sacrifice, then it would be hard for you to adjust as an online learner.

Online Education Can Be a Solitary Journey

Pursuing degrees through an online program can be a solitary journey and requires 100% self-motivation and accountability. Online education requires time, discipline, self-motivation, and a hard drive to succeed without the physical presence and support of professors and classmates typical in traditional classrooms. This entails finding resources on your own so you can do the tasks required. You need to spend a lot of time reading instructions and class materials so that you can do your assignments. No classmates are around for you to ask and clarify things you don't understand. Nobody will remind you of deadlines or explain how some parts of the assignment should be done. Unlike in traditional classrooms, where a professor will explain the information to you through extensive lectures, professors in online classes will post study materials or instructional videos, and it is up to you to read them and explain them to yourself. Online courses require heavy reading and writing assignments, as this is how you can be assessed whether you understand the lessons or not. Online learners call this self-teaching. I agree because self-teaching is the only way to learn in online education!

Many students in traditional classrooms can get by in passive mode. Their minds can wander during lectures, or they can be on their phones and computers with multiple tabs opened to browse that are totally irrelevant to the ongoing class discussions. Many college students just wing it through the passing grade because their names are included on a group project they hardly contributed to. They say that as long as you find good company on a traditional college campus, you are most likely to succeed. "C's get degrees," they say.

However, online students must be active learners! They would fail once they switch to a passive mode. If one misses the deadline for posting an answer to a discussion question, they get a zero. Compare that to a traditional classroom setting where one can hide behind a classmate's chair and avoid being called for a graded recitation or participation during class discussions. Online learners must comprehend what they read or listen to. They must be able to explain to themselves what they are learning. They must produce the work required to pass the course. And if there are group activities, the online platform can trace their contribution. Even in group projects, nowadays, modern technology helps professors track individual progress based on their input.

Online students also bemoan that there are no holidays, bad weather days, and sick days that would give them additional days off from school. The only time online students can get a break from online classes is if they request a break before they get enrolled in new classes. Unlike traditional classes, you cannot call in sick and be excused from the assignments. You need to work around sicknesses and other emergencies. You need to manage your personal, work, and academic schedules. Online education means resetting priorities and giving up some social events, such as parties, to make time for doing assignments. Many online students often overlook and do not expect that there will be temporary sacrifices such as these. Thus, they feel frustrations boiling over when the tremendous shift bothers their regular routines. But knowing these realities of online education may eliminate those frustrations.

Let's Wrap It Up!

Many online students feel overwhelmed when things get out of control. The dread and fear of failure are enough to trigger panic and anxiety attacks. Before you leave and walk away from pursuing your degree online, there are ways to reset your mindset. Identify what is causing your anxiety and panic attacks. Then, manage those triggers. Take control of things you can, surrender your worries to God, and flourish as an online student.

You are not too old to get that degree. Five years from now, you will still be five years older with or without a degree. You are not alone in this academic pursuit. There are thousands of others in America and across the globe who have ambitions like you. You want a better life, not just for yourself but also for the ones you love. So, when doubts arise and you begin wondering if you made a mistake enrolling in a course to get a degree, go back and look at your big picture. Unstuck yourself by recounting what you went through to even get started. Remember that everything has a cost, not just financial costs, but costs in time, health, relationships, and so on. Reflect on your misconceptions about online education, and accept the realities you are facing now.

Chapter 2

WHEN YOUR WHY MAKES YOU CRY

"And we know that in all things God works for the good of those who love him, who have been called according to his purpose." Romans 8:28 (NIV)

Why are you pursuing this online degree? Determining a clear answer to this question is the fuel for the rest of your academic journey. If your *why* does not make you cry, then it is not big enough. Your *why* must be big enough to fuel you through the finish line. In one of the schools I taught, we would have around 1,000 college freshmen at the start of the school year, but only 300 or less were on track to graduate on time. For online students, it is the same. More faculty are needed to teach the first-year sequence of courses due to a larger volume of enrollees compared to the core classes down the line.

I teach the first course online college students enroll in. Usually, I have 35 students on the first day of class. Before the first week ends, one or two would drop out. "Too many readings. Too many things to write!" was the first complaint. By the end of the course that lasted seven weeks, 7-10 students had dropped out, 4-6 failed, and only around 20 passed the course. Why is this so? As discussed in the previous chapter, they may have misconceptions and wrong expectations about pursuing college online. In addition to that, it is also probably because their *why* to pursue a college degree is not big enough. They do not have enough fuel to finish and surge all the way through to their graduation day.

Some barely last through the first course, dropping or failing it. Some online students' fuel lasts halfway, and some almost make it to the finish line, but not quite. I observed that the former is also true for doctoral learners who give up during their dissertation stage. They are almost there at the finish line! But somehow they hit a wall in the literature review, or the methodology chapter, so they give up. Before this random statistical overview scares you, remember that there are others who can power through to the finish line. And you can be one of them! So we will focus on the positive outcome rather than let the negative statistics scare us. If others can succeed, you can, too! Your mind is your limit.

And this is why your mind should hold on to the deep roots of a very clear *why*.

Why? Why are you pursuing this online degree? Until you get it into one statement, written hard and clear on your paper, for you and the world to see, you might not have enough fuel to make it to the finish line. Remember, if your *why* does not make you cry, it is not big enough to last you through to the finish line. OK, maybe the *cry* part is figurative. But for many people, their why could literally make them cry. Here are some *whys* people hold on to:

- A single mom wanted to get a better job that would allow her to provide better opportunities for her children.

- A new father wanted to find a better job opportunity that would allow him to stay locally, and stop being away from his family for months driving trucks across different states.

- A navy soldier does not want to become a homeless veteran, so he studies while on duty. Afterwards, he can look for employment opportunities as a regular citizen.

- A grandma wanted her grandchildren to value education so she aimed to be the first-generation college graduate in the family.

- A grandpa spent his whole life in the industry, but now that he retired, he wanted to spend his retirement years as a pastor in the local church and minister to young family men.

- A daughter wanted to be a nurse so she could take care of her ailing parents.

- A son wanted to be a licensed therapist so he could help his mother struggling with addiction.

- A firstborn of the family wanted to finish college to learn how to build a business and create job opportunities in the local community.

I have read thousands of *whys* throughout my almost 20 years of college teaching. When I was teaching in the Philippines, this was the first question I would ask my wide-eyed, hopeful, expectant, college freshmen in our first meeting. Why are you pursuing a college degree? And the most common answer was: "I want to go abroad, find a good-paying job, and lift my family from poverty."

This was the driving force of many average college students in the Philippines, and many of my former students have successfully reached this dream. These were the ones whose *whys* were big enough, and I enjoyed watching them walk across the graduation stage. Those whose *whys* involved something bigger than themselves were the ones that surpassed the difficult moments. On the other hand, there were some who were unsure of their *whys*, and with a shrug, would say, "My parents wanted me to," "So that my parents will continue supporting me," or "Because I don't know what to do with my life." Unsurprisingly, these were the ones that usually get crushed when the going gets tough and they end up taking longer to finish their degree or not at all.

Why is a very serious question. For 18-year-olds, going to college seems to be the next step after high school, the rite of passage into adulthood where dreams come true, or perhaps the only way to keep their parents' financial support coming. However, for adult learners pursuing any degree online, determining a clear answer to this question is a vital component that would fuel the drive to finish strong. You are no longer a hopeful yet naive 18-year-old. You are an adult, and you should know what you want. Writing a clear statement of your big *why* should not be a ridiculous idea, but it could be a difficult exercise. Not knowing your big *why* or having superficial reasons for pursuing a college degree is like running low on fuel or battery while on a long drive with no gas or charging station in sight.

Before you go further in this long drive, make sure you have enough fuel. If you are driving an electric vehicle, you also map out the charging stations along the way and plan your stops to charge to make sure you reach your destination safely. As an online learner, this means that your big *why* is clear to you and you are not wasting your time enrolling in college courses, hoping that you get enough passing scores to keep moving from one course to another until you graduate. The *why* could be your people, the driving force that motivates and keeps you inspired. It could be a dream of becoming an ideal person someday or perhaps obtaining possessions that you want to acquire.

What Is Your Big Why?

What is your big *why*? Think about people who motivate or inspire you to pursue your degree. Are these your parents whose dreams are for you to get a higher education? Are these your children for whom you are setting a good example? Or perhaps it is your spouse who encourages you to flourish because they see so much potential in you? Sometimes, the big *why* is not from other people. Sometimes, it is for yourself. Maybe there is something you want to become–a dream or an ambition that only higher education can bring. Do you want to be a teacher? A nurse? A doctor? An engineer? Aside from being motivated and inspired by other people, or ambitions to become someone, big *whys* can also stem from a deep desire and longing for a change of life, and higher education is the way to go.

Go beyond your present situation and visualize the big picture that will appear after you graduate. Make sure that your big *why* identifies your purpose beyond graduation. Your graduation is not the end in itself, but it is the ending needed to start a new beginning. Your degree is the springboard for the deeper meaning and purpose of your life. When your *why* involves other people, when it gives you meaning and purpose for your life after getting a degree, and when it is larger than yourself and goes beyond selfish reasons, then it is strong and big enough to fuel you through the finish line.

My Big WHYs

My big whys for each of my higher education degrees differ. My big why for getting a college degree was to help my parents send my siblings to college, too. At the end of this book, I added a section where I narrated my full story on why getting a college education is a way out of poverty in the Philippines. Since I graduated with a teaching degree from a small community college, I always had insecurities about my education. So for my Master's degree, my big *whys* were to get a job tenure and promotion. Then, I also secretly wanted to be on par with my colleagues who had graduated from prestigious universities in the Philippines. Knowing that I will be sticking to a career in higher education for the rest of my life, I always wanted to pursue a Ph.D. In "Before the Book," I shared the details on how I gave up on this dream. But that changed when I met my husband and he supported and encouraged me to go for it. There were many moments I wanted to give up, especially during the dissertation stage. But the thought of disappointing him kept me going.

Three Ways to Identify Your Big WHY

If you are still unsure what your big why is, now is the time to identify it. At the introduction of this section, I discussed visualizing the big picture. The big picture is the end game, the final scene that plays once you reach your goals. It may be the end of your academic success but all beginnings come from another's ending. So studying may be over for you, but it is the beginning of your life *after* you get your degree. This big picture is the culmination of all the tiny details in all of your hard work combined. But after you get your degree, and all the euphoria fades in the aftermath, it is your big *why* that would give meaning and purpose to the life you now have started to build.

Sadly, I have encountered many students who feel lost and do not know what to do after getting a degree. They wrapped up their identity in their studies, their excellent grades, and scholastic recognitions. Once this chapter in their life was over, they were like fish out of water. They don't know what to do with their life aside from looking for a job. Please do not allow this to happen to you.

Identify your big WHY now so you know your purpose after you graduate.

1. First, reflect on your personal goals. Why did you enroll in the first place? Why did you choose this degree that you are pursuing? What do you want to achieve by becoming this person after you graduate? Where do you want to be five years from now? How would this degree help you become that person, or bring you to where you want to be?

2. Next, identify what you value the most and what you are most passionate about. Are your values and passions aligned with the program you are pursuing? If not, are there avenues where you can channel these values and passions? One of my colleagues teaches communication courses, but he is passionate about building homes for other people. Building homes and teaching communication courses are not aligned to each other, but he volunteers at an organization that helps build houses for the less fortunate. So, there is an outlet outside of his career for him to channel the other thing he values most.

3. Lastly, consider your past, and your future. In the past, what was it that people say you are good at? If you have a hard time identifying what you are good at, ask several people and note what the similar answers are. Sometimes we fail to recognize what we are good at so ask around! Then, ask yourself where and what you want to be in the future? How do all these efforts you are exerting in your studies propel you towards where you see yourself in the future? Ask yourself, "How does this thing I am doing now contribute to where I want to be in the future?"

Look for the Signposts

Identifying the big *why* is crucial for an online student to stay motivated and focused throughout their studies. This will serve as your anchor and your true north so that you can keep going when the going gets tough. If at this point in your studies you discover that you don't have a big WHY for pursuing a degree, then maybe it is better to pause and reassess your situation. Because it is unwise to keep going when you know you are going in the wrong direction.

My husband and I were headed to Woods Canyon Lake up in Payson, Arizona. We were almost there when our GPS lost the signal. We started suspecting that we were going in the wrong direction when the paved road ended and we plunged into a dusty, dirt road. But instead of turning around, we kept driving all the while saying that we didn't remember going through that dirt road before. Then, we started noticing that there were no signs leading to that lake. However, we just kept driving.

Now, when you have a feeling that you are going in the wrong direction because you cannot see any road signs leading to the place where you want to go, then your instinct must be pretty accurate. There are no signposts because that is not the way to go. Finally, after about three or four more miles of driving on that dusty dirt road, we decided to turn around. Guess what? When we turned around, we started seeing signs directing the way to the lake. Later, we figured that we missed the turn to the right. We kept going straight, thus the signs leading to the lake disappeared because it was already behind us.

In most of life's situations, it is the same. When you feel that you are headed in the wrong direction, then maybe you really are. So, it is time to stop and reassess your life and what you are doing. It is possible that big WHYs change while you are in the middle of your academic journey, so there is no point in continuing if you no longer see the purpose behind your endeavors.

Right after college, I enrolled in a master's program. My goal was to become a school principal and have my own preschool. Two years into the program, I paused my studies to participate in an international exchange program that brought me to the US in 2004 for the first time. The international experience and cultural exposure changed me so much that when I got back home in the Philippines after a year, I could no longer see myself being a school principal. Furthermore, I can no longer see myself building my own preschool because my passion shifted from elementary education to higher education.

If a shift like this happens to you right when you are halfway done with your program, please be reminded that this is totally OK. This is not a failure. You have two options: Just finish your program for the sake of finishing what you started before pivoting into that shift, or quit and never look back. Shifting or pivoting while you are halfway done could be an opportunity to recalibrate and resharpen yourself. Maybe the shift, or making that u-turn, will help you see the signposts again. Maybe, like me, you will find another set of big *whys* that will take you where you are supposed to be.

Called for a Purpose

God has a purpose for you. Whenever you think that you've failed or messed up, always remember that all things will work for the good of those who love the Lord. You are called according to His purpose. Sometimes, it is hard to even believe that God has amazing plans for our lives. 1 Corinthians 2:9 (NKJV) says that, "Eye has not seen, nor ear heard, nor have entered into the heart of man the things which God has prepared for those who love Him." We cannot imagine or fathom the fullness of God's purpose for us from where we are standing. We need to trust Him that He will guide us through every step of the way. So, if you are not sure what your big WHYs are, or what this degree that you are pursuing is for, then ask God to show you.

Let's Wrap It Up!

Always remember your big *why*. If your *why* doesn't make you cry, then it is not big enough. Your big WHY is the fuel that will push you through the finish line. If you don't have at least one, then now is the time to write one. Reflect on your personal goals, what you are most passionate about, what it was in the past that people said you were good at, and what you see yourself to be in the future. The answers to these prompts can help you identify your big WHY.

Chapter 3

HOLD TIGHT— ANCHORED IN GOD'S WORD

> *"I will instruct you and teach you in the way you should go; I will counsel you with my eye upon you." Psalm 32:8 (ESV)*

When the storms of life rock your boat, you need an anchor to hold it in place. When a boat or a ship is in the middle of the sea during the storm and it is not anchored, it will be tossed back and forth. It can capsize or break apart, endangering the lives of people onboard. Likewise, when desperations and frustrations hit you during the course of your academic journey, you need to go back to God's Word and anchor yourself into His promises.

First of all, I want to be clear that God loves you and cares for you no matter what your educational background is. With or without a college degree, He already loves you just the way you are. Whether you are young or old, a fast learner or average, determined or discouraged, He knows you fully well and sees beyond that facade that you display to impress other people. He knows your past, your present, and your future.

God knows your intentions and inspirations. He knows what motivates you and what demotivates you. He sees your joy and happiness, sorrow and sadness. He sees you in your struggles, in your fears, and in your anxiety. He sees every single tear you wipe away, and His heart goes out to you when He hears you bawling and wailing in desperation as you try to get through an assignment in the middle of the night. He sees you when you are so tired and all you wanted was to finish your academic tasks and get some sleep.

Ah, yes. There are moments like that! I had plenty of those, too. That's why I held this verse tight, my assurance that God cares. "You have kept count of my tossings; put my tears in your bottle. Are they not in your book?" (Psalm 56:8, ESV) This verse tells me that God sees my "tossings" or restlessness, frustrations, anxiety, efforts, and tears. "Keeping my tears in a bottle," means they are precious to Him, and He will not let it go to waste. "Are they not in your book?" for me means that God sees and keeps records of my struggles. He doesn't shrug them off carelessly, ignores them, or forgets about them, but they were all carefully noted. The sacrifices I made for my studies are known to God, and He can do with them whatever He pleases.

> *"You have kept count of my tossings; put*
> *my tears in your bottle. Are they not in your book?"*
> *Psalm 56:8 (ESV)*

Nevertheless, do not ever think that God would love and respect you more or you will become His favorite child once you get your degree. Establish this truth in your heart and mind. Let that sink in for a while. You are fully known and fully loved by your Creator, the God of this universe, just as you are right now. This degree will not change how God sees and loves you. Hence, consider this degree as an offering of thanksgiving for everything that He has done in your life so that through it, you can serve Him more.

> *"But God chose the foolish things of the world to shame the wise;*
> *God chose the weak things of the world to shame the strong."*
> *1 Corinthians 1:27 (NIV)*

Therefore, your perspectives of other people who did not have a chance to get a higher education degree should be one of respect and high regard. God is no respecter of persons based on educational achievement. He can use anyone, educated or not, to bring Him glory and honor and carry out His will for humanity. In fact, 1 Corinthians 1: 27 (NIV) says, "But God chose the foolish things of the world to shame the wise; God chose the weak things of the world to shame the strong." This verse should humble us and remind us that without Him, we are nothing. God looks into our hearts and from there, He can use us in wonderful and mighty ways. So, when you get your degree, don't go to God, feeling entitled that you are deserving of better things in life.

"God, give me a better job."

"God, give me a better house."

"God, give me a better life. I have a higher education degree!"

No. What you should be saying to God is:

"God, how can I serve you better now that I am more equipped?"

"God, where do you want to use me?"

"God, am I at the very center of your will right now?"

"Here I am, Lord. Send me!"

> *"...here I am. Send me." Isaiah 6:8 (ESV)*

God Used Educated People in the Bible

Albeit, there are several Bible characters that were educated, and God used them mightily to fulfill the purposes of His kingdom. Two of them are Moses from the Old Testament, and Paul from the New Testament. "Moses was educated in all the wisdom of the Egyptians and was powerful in speech and action," Acts 7:22 (NIV) This is interpreted by Bible scholars as *higher education* at that time. Ancient Egyptian education included lessons in areas such as language, leadership, mathematics, astronomy, and medicine. As you probably know, God called Moses to lead the Israelites out of bondage and brought them safely to the threshold of the Promised Land. Perhaps the knowledge he gained from his formal education helped him become the leader that he was.

Paul, from the New Testament, was a well-educated and highly popular Pharisee. He had a thorough understanding of the law, or the first five books of the Bible. Although he did not believe that Jesus was the Messiah at first, Jesus revealed Himself to Paul in a special way. Eventually, God used Him as a missionary to the *Gentiles*[3] and the early church grew as the gospel was preached. He is the author of many books in the New Testament which connected the truths from the Old Testament to prove that Jesus is the Messiah that had long been prophesied and waited for by the Jews. He was able to explain to the Gentiles the good news of salvation for humanity. Without his educational background, I don't think he would have been able to write and expound the truths of God's plan for salvation–especially to the Gentiles.

Jesus had 12 disciples; most of them were fishermen, and were not as educated as Paul. Even still, they were used mightily by Jesus in His ministry, even after He returned to heaven. However, only a handful of them such as Peter, James, and John were able to write books that became part of the New Testament. To drive home the point, God can use your education for greater impact in this generation and the generations to come even beyond your lifetime!

Is It God's Will for Me to Study?

"Is it God's will for me to study?" By all means, the answer to this question is a loud, "Yes!" The Bible is a profound source of wisdom and guidance for all areas of life, including education. It is filled with messages that encourage learning, growth, and productivity. From the beginning when God created Adam and Eve and placed them in the Garden of Eden, His first instructions were to "be fruitful and increase in number" (Genesis 1:28, NIV). And for the garden, they should "work it and take care of it." (Genesis 2:15, NIV) God is a God of multiplication! He does not want you to be stagnant.

Do you remember the parable of the talents? This story is found in Matthew 25:14-28. A master entrusted money to his servants. To the first

---

3   Gentiles are people who are not Jewish during Bible times.

one, he gave five. To the second one, he gave two, and to the third, he gave one. After a long time, the master returned and asked them to report back about the money he left them. The one who got five doubled it to ten. The second one who got two also doubled it to four. The third one who got one buried it and came back with the same amount. The master got so angry and called him a wicked and lazy servant, then ordered that he be banished away. You see, whatever God has given you—skills, talents, knowledge, etc. He wants you to multiply that! He wants you to flourish!

In today's world, the most common path to success is by obtaining higher education. Take note that I said, the "most common path." I want to clarify that it is not the only path, and it is not a guarantee for success either. You will hear about a lot of people with college, master's, and even doctoral degrees who could not find a job, nor establish their own business as a source of income and livelihood. What does this mean for you? Do not put your trust and hope in your education. You need to be open and trust that God will use you. Your education is just a way for you to be equipped for God's purposes in your life. This perspective will relieve you from a lot of stress.

I went to a Christian school when I was in elementary, and this verse was always on display in our classroom: "Study to show thyself approved unto God, a workman that needeth not to be ashamed, rightly dividing the word of truth." (2 Timothy 2:15, KJV) Does this mean we have to study to gain God's approval? No. Remember, we already established that God loves and cares for us no matter what.

But what does it mean that we should study to be approved by God? Look at the verse this way. When I was nine years old, I learned how to take care of my baby siblings. My sister and my brother were two years apart. I *studied* how to change diapers, lift a newborn baby from the crib, feed them, rock them to sleep, put them down gently so they wouldn't wake up, etc. I *studied* how to do these tasks even though I was a child myself. When my mom saw that I had learned how to do these tasks carefully, she *approved* and trusted me to take care of my baby siblings even without her supervision. On the other hand, I have two other siblings, a five-year-old and a two-year-old, who were *not approved* to do these things. Does this mean that my mother loved them less since she did not approve of them to take care of the babies? No. My mother loves us all the same, but I got approval since I *studied* how to do those tasks right. Now, even if I am the oldest, if I did not take the time to learn how to do them right, I don't think my mother would have trusted me to do those tasks. This is how I interpret this line from the verse, "Study to show thyself approved unto God...." God would *approve* you to do greater tasks for His purposes, but you have to *study.*

When we commit to learning, we align ourselves with God's plan for us, which, according to Jeremiah 29:11 (NIV), is "to prosper you and not to harm you, plans to give you hope and a future." Just think. God already has a plan for you. His plan is to prosper you, give you hope, and a future. If you think that you are not along the lines of prospering, having hope, nor having a bright future in sight, you need to ask God how you can align yourself to His will so that His plans for you will unfold. Clearly, if you feel that you are stuck at the moment in circumstances beyond your control, it is not the destination God has planned for you. You need to ask Him how you can get out of it so you can find yourself at the center of His plans. You need to trust His perfect timing and be patient in obedience to His Word.

The Enemy Steals, Kills, and Destroy

Jesus Himself, in John 10:10 (NKJV), tells us that He came so that we "may have life... and have it more abundantly." Take a moment to reflect on that. Jesus came, not only to save us and give us eternal life. Between the delight in salvation that we have in Jesus today, and the eternal life that we will have in heaven with Him, is the life we are living right now on this earth. We are in this small dash from the year we were born and the day we will die. But, no matter how short or long our dash is in earthly years, the good news of salvation includes, not just living a life to survive the in-between, but to have life abundantly.

However, it is important to note that the first part of John 10:10 (NKJV) also said, "The thief does not come except to steal, and to kill, and to destroy..." Think of these words in order. First, the thief, Satan, will come and then steal. Steal your dreams. Steal your purpose in life. Steal your joy, peace, and love. Steal your motivation to improve yourself, and act on the plans and purposes of God for you. Once he has stolen these things from you, he will kill, then destroy. He could destroy your physical body, crush your emotions, and ruin your spiritual life.

In ancient times, when there were battles, the enemy did not only kill, but they also destroyed everything that belonged to their opponent. They burned the cities, animals, crops, homes, etc. to the ground. This was to make sure that if anyone escaped and survived, they would no longer have anything to return to. Satan, our enemy, is the same. He will steal, then kill, then destroy the abundant life that Jesus came for you to have.

What if God's plan for you is to get a college degree? But then, that one professor gave you a failing grade on an assignment? With raging tears and an exploding heart, you threw your hands up in the air and crashed your laptop to the ground. You gave up and walked away from your academic journey. I have met a lot of students, some of them my own classmates, who were almost there at the finish line. But they got so beaten and tired that they gave up.

Next time, when you encounter difficulties in life that affect your academic pursuits, pause and pray. Perhaps this is an attack from the enemy. Do you know that if you give up, you are allowing the enemy to triumph in his plot to steal, kill, and destroy everything that God set up for you? Instead of crashing your laptop and grinding it to a pulp on the ground, you should fall on your knees and beg God for mercy. Beg God to help you through, to give you strength, peace, calm, and wisdom in this very diffiult and discouraging moment. You need to beg God for His favor and grace to keep going.

Nothing Can Separate Us from God's Love

To think that Satan's intent is to kill, steal, and destroy every good and perfect gift that God has for us is scary. How can we thwart that off? Remember, that is only the first part of the verse. The second part has the answer. "...but I have come that they may have life, and that they may have it more abundantly." (John 10:10, NKJV) Jesus is the answer. Having Jesus in your life is the only way you can be protected from Satan's evil schemes. Romans 8:35-39 listed down all the possible, awful things that could happen, and it clearly said that none of these things can separate us from the love of God which is in Christ Jesus. We are more than conquerors through Jesus who loved us!

"Who shall separate us from the love of Christ? Shall trouble or hardship or persecution or famine or nakedness or danger or sword?

As it is written:

'For your sake we face death all day long;
we are considered as sheep to be slaughtered.'

No, in all these things we are more than conquerors through him who loved us. For I am convinced that neither death nor life, neither angels nor demons, neither the present nor the future, nor any powers, neither height nor depth, nor anything else in all creation, will be able to separate us from the love of God that is in Christ Jesus our Lord." (NIV)

What Do These Have to Do with Your Study?

Armed with these truths from God's Word, you should walk boldly and confidently, worthy of the calling by which you are called. What is the degree that you are pursuing? Are you going to be a teacher, a psychologist, a minister, a health professional, etc.? Whatever it is, that is your calling. Walk in a manner worthy of that calling, armed with the truths of God's Word. Whenever you face obstacles and curveballs in your academic journey, declare God's truths over it, and be assured that you can overcome them all victoriously in Jesus' name! Financial hardships, health crises, technological challenges, relationship woes, and family matters are all examples of situations that are not academic in nature and yet would impact your academic performance. Do not get distracted or discouraged by these!

"I... urge you to walk in a manner worthy
of the calling to which you have been called."
Ephesians 4:1 (ESV)

Declare that Jesus has come to give you an abundant life, and His plans for you are to prosper and not to harm you, to give you hope and a future. Declare that nothing can separate you from God's love, no matter how awful your situation is, and that you will continue walking in a manner worthy of the calling by which you are called despite all the obstacles and curveballs that Satan throws your way to distract you. Go boldly to the throne of grace and obtain mercy and grace from our Lord Jesus. Always ask Him for help in time of need.

"Let us then with confidence draw near to the throne of grace,
that we may receive mercy and find grace to help in time of need."
Hebrews 4:16 (ESV)

During the course of your academic pursuits many things can happen that can knock you off and derail you from your successful undertaking. This is not to scare you off, but this is the reality of life. I have many students, especially during the COVID-19 pandemic years, who lost their loved ones, got terribly sick, got evicted from their homes, struggled with mental health, or went into financial crises. Why a good God would allow these terrible things to happen is not for us to question. Jesus Himself said that in this world we will have troubles. But we need to take heart because He has overcome. And as His children, we can also overcome because God's grace is sufficient.

"I have said these things to you, that in me you may have peace. In the
world you will have tribulation. But take heart; I have overcome the
world." John 16:33 (ESV)

An Atheist Who Could Not Resist

Eric was one of my students during the pandemic. I remember him because he wrote me a long message on the very first day of our online class. He said that he'd just been evicted from his apartment and had become homeless. He went to a nearby coffee shop to get an internet connection, but slept with his belongings on the pavement. Homelessness was just a cherry on top of all his problems, a result of one bad circumstance after another. This included losing a job, getting a divorce, and losing a court battle for child custody. All these wore him down mentally. He was exhausted to do assignments!

Some of his problems were admittedly his fault, and some were beyond his control. I talked to him over the phone and tried to encourage him with the same Bible verses I discussed earlier in this chapter. He was ready to quit school, but I promised I would work with him if he tried his best. There were many late submissions and some missed assignments. Giving consideration to his predicament, I gave minimal deductions or none at all to all his late submissions just so he could pull a passing grade. He expressed apologies and thoughts on giving up. But I told him that he couldn't give up this one good thing going on in his life.

Before our class ended, he said he'd found a new place to live and a new job. But he said something else that I will never forget. He said he was an atheist and did not believe in God. But the Bible verses I shared with him sounded so powerful that he could not bring himself to tell me to stop. He appreciated that I prayed for him because he felt a sense of peace and assurance that everything would be OK.

When I was talking to Eric, sharing all those Bible verses and praying to encourage him, I did not know that he was an atheist, or I would have been very cautious. But I'm glad I didn't know. I'm glad God's Word had a powerful presence in his dark season, and it was my prayer that Eric would believe in God one day. I've never heard back from him since then. But I know God's got him! If an atheist could not resist the power of God's Word because they found peace and assurance in them, how much more can it do for you if you are a believing Christian?

Let's Wrap It Up!

The word of God is powerful. As an online student, you can be resilient if your core foundation is grounded and anchored in God's Word. Always remember that God loves you despite knowing you fully well. There is nothing you can hide from Him, and despite all the messy parts of your life, God loves and cares for you. This academic pursuit, this degree you are aiming to have, is an offering of thanksgiving to Him and for everything that He has done in your life. If God can use educated people in the Bible such as Moses and Paul to accomplish His plans and purposes, pray that God will also use your education to bring greater impact in building His kingdom on earth.

Treasure God's word in your heart. We should study to show ourselves approved unto God and not be ashamed. His plan for you is to prosper, and not be harmed; to give you hope and a future. Satan's intent may be to steal, kill, and destroy, but Jesus came not only to give us eternal life but so that we can live an abundant life here on earth. In Jesus, nothing can separate us from the love of God. We can boldly come to His throne of grace and ask for help in times of need. In this world, we will have troubles. But we can take heart knowing that our Savior has overcome!

Part 2

CHOOSE

Focus: Choosing a Life Aligned with Values and Wellness

"I call Heaven and Earth to witness against you today: I place before you Life and Death, Blessing and Curse. Choose life so that you and your children will live. And love GOD, your God, listening obediently to him, firmly embracing him." Deuteronomy 30:19 (MSG)

Due to poor planning and horrible time management, I put myself into a place of indecision. Should I go to Singapore for the weekend, or finish a major paper for my graduate studies? I bought a very cheap $30 flight from Manila to Singapore when it went on sale many months ago. But because of procrastination, poor planning, horrible time management, a very busy season at work, and many other excuses, I did not finish a major paper due that weekend for my graduate studies.

In this moment of indecision, questions popped into my head. What is my goal? To graduate, of course. Which is my priority, to travel or study? Which one would bring me closer to my goal? I was at a crossroads. After mentally battling it out, the choice was clear. I knew I needed to forego that cheap, nonrefundable ticket and stay home for the weekend to finish my paper. I had to keep my tears from falling as I tried to quiet the taunting voice in my head saying, "You could be strolling in Sentosa taking nice pictures right now while drinking a cold latte. And tonight, you're supposed to enjoy *laksa*[4] for dinner. But look at you, stuck in your apartment, writing a paper no one but your professor will read."

Such is the life of online students. We are constantly exerting efforts, making conscious choices that would lead us closer to our academic goals. Close your eyes for a moment and imagine you are standing at a crossroads. On your left is the languishing path, and on your right is the flourishing path. Which would you choose? In Deuteronomy 30:19 (MSG), God says that He will "...place before you life and death, blessing and curse. Choose life..."

Choose! The *choose* part is not always easy. Like the international trip I had to give up, the flourishing path is not always fun and inviting, making it harder to choose. Sometimes, the way to flourishing means getting down to the nitty gritty stuff and working hard in isolation. Now, think of the choices you make every day concerning your studies. When you are doing your schoolwork, you are constantly choosing between languishing and flourishing until you get it done. Each nanosecond moment constantly shifts between life and death, blessing and cursing as distractions arise to keep you from doing your work. You need to be conscious, cautious, and committed to keep choosing the path that leads to flourishing at every waking moment.

When you are crushed by the stress of your job, and you still have assignments to do, the languishing path beckons you to throw a pity party. The flourishing path cajoles you to stay positive and stay on track never giving up. When you go home after a 12-hour shift at your job to a house in disarray, and your children are hungry, screaming both for dinner and loving attention from you, the languishing path waves at you to throw a fit and scream back at them. However, the flourishing path whispers, "Put dinner in the oven, hug and love your children until they are calmed down, feed them, and put them to bed happy. Then tidy up at least a little corner of your house, throw in some laundry, take a hot shower, and no matter how tired you are, just for one hour more, do one task or part of a bigger assignment so that you can keep moving forward in your academic journey."

---

4   *Laksa* in Singapore is a popular, flavorful noodle soup dish, particularly known for its rich and creamy coconut curry broth.

The languishing path says, "Complain, cry, this world is not fair."

The flourishing path interjects, "Cry, it is OK. But rise up, dry your tears, and fix your crown. Smile, and find things to be grateful for."

The academic journey is different for everyone because each person's situation is unique. This is your personal journey, and you have to own it. You need to actively choose the path to flourishing at every waking hour when you find your gaze getting sidetracked or your faith wavering because the moment's challenges are insurmountable. You must be aware that you are writing the story of your academic journey.

Now, to be actively choosing the path to flourishing, you must understand its different domains. Think of flourishing like a machine. When you know the different parts of the machine, it is easier to identify where the problem is coming from when it malfunctions. When something sounds odd or not working, you don't throw away the whole machine. Maybe there are just some parts that need to be fixed, and the whole machine will work like new again. I remember a time when our washing machine broke and my husband asked if it was time to buy a new one. I suggested that we look if it was still covered by the warranty. Sure enough, it was! Soon, the mechanic was replacing some parts and he was able to fix it. It happened around five years ago, and to this day, our washing machine is still working.

When you think you're languishing, don't assume that your whole life is a mess. Maybe there are just some parts that are broken and need fixing. You can take a hard look at your life and identify which areas of flourishing need some upgrades, repairs, sharpening, or polishing. Just because you have a hard situation in life does not mean that you cannot flourish.

Flourishing. Mental images may flash across your mind as you hear the word flourishing. As an online learner, a life flourishing for you may look like finding balance in your time spent studying and socializing, finishing assignments way before the deadlines, obtaining a perfect GPA of 4.0, having a happy marriage, having well-disciplined, adorable children, or getting a job promotion all on top of studying online! However, after graduation, these parameters of flourishing change.

A flourishing life for you may be about passing the state's board exam or licensure test, getting a more decent-paying job, getting a nicer car, renting a better apartment, and paying off student loans. A flourishing life after graduation may be a picture of having more quality time with your spouse, being more present at your children's activities, volunteering in communities, serving in the church ministries, acquiring properties, establishing businesses, advancing in your career, and so on. Meanwhile, if you are in your twilight years, the picture of a flourishing life is staying in good health, having great relationships with your children and grandchildren, being generous, not fearing death, and modeling an abundant life of happiness. All of these are typical pictures of flourishing that are secretly captured in our mental images when we hear this word.

But what is *flourishing*?

Flourishing refers to a state of well-being, growth, and success in various aspects of life. It encompasses a sense of purpose, positive emotions, positive relationships, personal growth, and the achievement of goals. Flourishing is often considered a holistic concept, encompassing physical, mental, emotional, and social well-being. Some researchers argue that flourishing is the highest level of human well-being. Otherwise, they are languishing, struggling, or floundering. Researchers such as Diener, Rautenbach, Keyes, and VanderWeele have tried to encapsulate flourishing by inventing survey instruments that measure the different flourishing domains in different contexts of human life. In this book, I focused on VanderWeele's domains of flourishing.

The Flourishing Measure,[5] a survey instrument created by VanderWeele in 2017, has six domains. They are happiness and life satisfaction, mental and physical health, meaning and purpose, character and virtue, close social relationships, and financial and material stability. All these domains of the Flourishing Measure are similar to the domains other researchers have included in their survey instruments, except for financial and material stability. VanderWeele argued that financial and material stability is essential to flourishing because it sustains other areas

---

5   *The Flourishing Measure* by Tyler VanderWeele is a questionnaire designed to assess an individual's level of human flourishing, encompassing six key domains: happiness and life satisfaction, mental and physical health, meaning and purpose, character and virtue, close social relationships, and financial and material stability. https://hfh.fas.harvard.edu/measuring-flourishing

of flourishing over a more extended period of time. This is the reason why I chose this instrument to measure flourishing both in my dissertation and in this book because I believe that finances play a part in flourishing.

Likewise, even the Bible talks about human flourishing. From the Garden of Eden, we can see the heart of God, willing that the humans He created flourish. He told Adam and Eve to go and multiply and replenish the earth. He set them up for success, and gave them all the necessary tools to flourish. Unfortunately, Adam and Eve sinned, and since then, the world has been spiraling downward. That's why Jesus came to save us and give us hope and protection from the destruction this world is headed to. Jesus declared that even though the enemy has come to steal, kill, and destroy, He has come to give us life and life to the fullest.

Hence, the following chapters discussing these domains of flourishing posited by VanderWeele, also include Scriptures that reveal what God's Word has to say about each aspect of flourishing. No matter what mental image of flourishing flashes through your mind, the following discussions on the domains of human flourishing would provide a good baseline for having a deeper understanding of this topic that is very near to the heart of God.

Flourishing is a *choice!*

Chapter 4

THE MYTH OF "HAPPY ENOUGH"

"I know that there is nothing better for people than to be happy and to do good while they live." Ecclesiastes 3:12 (NIV)

Pursue your degree from a happy and satisfied disposition, not from a grumpy, frazzled, and exhausted posture. Overall, how happy and satisfied are you? Take some time to reflect and rate your level of happiness and life satisfaction with 10 as the highest score, and 0 as the lowest. I want you to look deeply from within. Stop for a minute, and look hard at yourself. Think of your overall happiness and life satisfaction including areas of your spiritual life, marriage or romance, and other personal goals aside from that degree you are working on. Don't just rate your level of happiness and life satisfaction within the confines of your academic experiences, because all areas of your life are connected, impacting each other. Happiness and life satisfaction are the first indications of flourishing.

The Quest for Happiness and Life Satisfaction

The study of human flourishing is deeply rooted in research about happiness and life satisfaction. As more factors are discovered about what makes humans happy and satisfied, the term flourishing emerged, and *happiness and life satisfaction* became only one of the many domains that constitute human flourishing. Happiness and life satisfaction indicates the positive emotion that leads to contentment and enough passion to continue developing and improving one's full potential.

Happiness and joy. We often use the terms *happiness* and *joy* interchangeably. While these two words share similar concepts about positive and elated emotion, there are subtle differences. The nature and source of happiness are dependent on external circumstances or situations. *Happenings.* It is dependent on what is happening around us. On the other hand, joy arises from within despite negative circumstances or situations. For example, failing a course is not a happy experience. However, your joy remains when you realize that the reason for failing your course was because you prioritized your children when they were sick. Now that they are well, you can give yourself grace from this failure knowing that you failed not because you were lazy and irresponsible. You may have failed a course, but you did not fail as a parent.

There are many sources of happiness: romance, a new baby, promotion at work, accolades and praises, getting straight A's and a 4.0 GPA, vacations, achievements, etc. Happiness fluctuates, is temporary, and is fleeting, while joy is deeply rooted and long-lasting because it is based on inner peace and contentment. Happiness is largely dependent on factors such as relationships, achievements, or material possessions; take these external factors away and the feeling wanes. Joy, however, is connected to the inner state that arises from gratitude, purpose, connection, spirituality, or love. Happiness can lead to a temporary boost of positive mood and overall well-being but may not sustain a long-term fulfillment. Meanwhile, joy has a deeper sense of fulfillment and can provide resilience and strength during tough times making it more enduring and transformative.

When I was a student, I had many outbursts of happy moments. Getting an A for an assignment, or as a final grade for a course; praises or positive feedback from my teacher; slaying a great presentation; publishing an article based on an assignment in a journal publication, and meeting an online classmate in person were all happy moments. These are all positive experiences, but they don't last. The next assignment with a deadline comes again, a new course starts, another presentation is due, and who knows when I'd get great feedback from another teacher. And getting an article published in a journal only happened once!

My friend, Pearl and I were writing our dissertations at around the same time. Whenever one of us would accomplish a small milestone, such as passing the proposal defense, we would go out for lunch and celebrate: Good food, and delightful desserts paired with tea or coffee. It was pure happiness. But guess what? The next milestone was waiting to be achieved, and our emotions would go on a rollercoaster ride again filled with frustrations, anxiety, and discouragement before we got another dose of that happiness.

Despite this repetitive cycle of emotions, I found strength and unexplainable joy when I counted my blessings and was grateful for the small progress even though the road ahead had no end in sight. I would think of the many times God brought me out of challenging milestones such as a student teaching in college, passing the board exam, getting my first job, being chosen as an *IVEP*[6] participant from the Philippines, and the list goes on. Looking back, the dissertation experience reminds me of the verse from Nehemiah 8:10 (NIV) "...Do not grieve, for the joy of the Lord is your strength."

When you turn your thoughts to the Lord and think of all the wonderful things He has done in your life that brought you to where you are right now, you will feel this *joy* that I am talking about. It is this kind of joy that lasts and pushes you to keep going forward. If you bring to remembrance all of God's faithfulness in your life and how He has brought you this far, you know that He can bring you to the place where He wants you to be. Surely, you still have far to go. But looking back, you have already gone so far! With this renewed mindset, you will feel

---

6   The International Volunteer Exchange Program (IVEP) is a yearlong volunteer work and cultural exchange opportunity for Christian adults ages 18-30 living outside the U.S. or Canada. This is one of the many programs sponsored by Mennonite Central Committee based in Akron, Pennsylvania. https://mcc.org/get-involved/volunteer/ivep

encouraged knowing that the Lord will also bring you out of your current season victoriously just as He has done in the past, even if the road ahead looks treacherous and cumbersome.

Life satisfaction. For online learners, life satisfaction may be a challenging quest. The constant academic workload and consistent pressure can take a toll, bringing you frustrations, fear, anguish, and regret. Getting a higher education degree *online* can pose mental health problems, financial difficulties, and feelings of isolation. Mental health problems can develop when there's a constant awareness that you need to keep your life together. This means that you cannot just focus on your studies and keep getting A's. You also need to take care of your family, love your spouse, maintain friendships, participate in social events, and thrive in your full-time career. And then, of course, financial challenges can arise. Some have student loans to cover tuition fees and many others have to keep working full-time to cover life's expenses. Dealing with all of these can feel very isolating. The more you balance the many aspects of your life, the easier it is to feel life satisfaction. But take note: It is *hard!*

The Case of Montecarlos and Amores

I know a lot of successful academicians. They have published a lot of research in journal publications, presented their scientific discoveries at conferences, and are well-known in their field of expertise. They bury themselves in their academic work and each accomplishment brings them a shining moment. When they are on stage, the world envies them. However, since I know some of them personally, I would say that they are not to be envied at all because they are as broken as anyone could be.

Most are not living a balanced life, and they have broken relationships, health problems, and are socially disconnected. Dr. Montecarlos got her Ph.D. before she turned 30, was married and had three kids when I met her. She was churning out a lot of publications in a year, getting invitations for international conference presentations from different countries, earning grants and scholarships, and getting paid a lot of money for her work. Her children were young and cute. Her husband would occasionally come with her to the campus, and I would see displays of affection. It was a perfect picture of a happy, satisfying life. I looked at her with envy and wondered how she got it all together at such a young age.

A few more years rolled by, and I got to know her more from our occasional chats. I began to realize that her life may not be that ideal after all because she doesn't know how to have fun! She had no girlfriends to hang out with. Or maybe I should say, she didn't want to hang out with anybody and cultivate friendships because she was always secluded in her office doing research day and night. Her identity was wrapped and buried in her academic work.

Slowly, I witnessed cracks appearing in her picture-perfect life until they became too much that her life crumbled away. First, her health declined rapidly due to her sedentary lifestyle. She has no routines for physical exercise. She never cooks for her family, and they would either eat out or have pre-cooked microwavable food. She also boasts of getting only 3-4 hours of sleep every day (no wonder she can write and publish so much)! Eventually, these habits gave her obesity, high blood pressure, diabetes, kidney stones, and carpal tunnel syndrome. She has such weak, brittle bones that incidences of her tripping or falling on the ground became frequent. One time, she fell and broke her ankle. Another time, she broke her arm.

Life moved on for both of us, and I have not heard from her in a long time. I asked a common friend recently if she knew or had heard anything about her. What I found out did not surprise me. She is now single, but divorced thrice. None of her children inherited her love for the academe.

"What do her children do?" I asked with curiosity.

"Oh, they hang around in her house and play video games," my friend replied nonchalantly. "None of them has a job, and they all depend on her for financial support."

I sighed. Her children are all adults by now.

Sometimes, you don't have to wait for things to unfold in your life to reflect *on* life. You can look at other people's lives and learn from them. Dr. Sienna Amores is a close friend of mine. After she got married in her mid-thirties, she slowed down in her academic career to prioritize life outside the academe. She took the minimum teaching load to keep her full-time job, but refused any schedule that would take her away from getting her children to school early in the morning or getting home in time for dinner. She stopped doing research, writing books, and doing conference presentations. Many of her colleagues shook their heads and thought that she was wasting her Ph.D. by getting stagnant in her career.

"Your children will grow up even without you doting on them," one of them said.

"You can still take care of your family without sacrificing your career," another chimed in.

These concerns from well-meaning colleagues did not faze her. Years passed and today her children are excelling in school. She told me that marriage and family life are not always easy. But by God's grace, they are content and satisfied with their simple lifestyle.

"I can go back to doing research, writing books, presenting at conferences, and all that academic stuff when my children have grown and flown. They will only be young once, and I want to see and enjoy their milestones while I can," she softly said, searching my eyes for understanding. In response, I nodded with admiration and agreed that she was doing the right thing.

Reflecting on the lives of Dr. Montecarlos and my friend Sienna was a sobering experience for me. Both of them were in pursuit of life satisfaction. The former thought life satisfaction was found in excellent academic achievements, while the latter knew that life must be balanced in all aspects. Personally, I think that many people tend to wrap their identity in their academic work because it is their comfort zone, their safety blanket. They neglect the other aspects of their lives that they need to nourish to truly flourish.

Hedonia and Eudaimonia

Do you know that there are two types of happiness and joy? The academic terminologies for these are *hedonia* and *eudaimonia*. Hedonia is happiness found in pleasure, enjoyment, comfort, and absence of distress. Some examples of hedonic happiness are going to a spa, dining out with friends, or dancing at a party after getting a good grade on a difficult test. On the other hand, eudaimonia is the highest good for human beings, a way of functioning. Eudaimonia ascribes to the joy found or evidenced by growth, meaning, authenticity, and excellence. Some examples of eudaimonic happiness are smiling at a stranger, helping an old lady cross the street, bringing doughnuts for your colleagues in the office, volunteering at a homeless shelter, or sponsoring a child's education in a third-world country.

Picture your graduation day. You are in a nice new dress, new shoes, beautiful makeup, and are sporting a gorgeous hairdo. Your academic robe, medals, honor cords, and cap are all in place. Your family and friends are with you in the venue, all cheering and clapping as your name is called and you walk across the graduation stage. After the ceremony, you all head out for a party, and once again, you are the center of attention and congratulatory remarks. The joy and happiness are insurmountable as you beam and glow with pride. You did it! This is a pure, hedonic experience!

But the following day, you all return home. You put your new dress in the wash, your shoes in the closet, and your academic robe is either returned to the providers or sent to the dry cleaners. You wash the makeup off your face and undo your hair before showering. The noise of congratulatory remarks die down and everyone returns to their normal routines. The day after graduation to many students can be depressing, but not for you. You are going to update your resume, write a book, and start a business. You have a bigger purpose than your degree, and you are on it right away. Graduating and getting a degree is hedonic happiness, but having a purpose after graduation where you will use your degree for the betterment of your community is pure eudaimonic joy!

Does God Want Me to Be Happy?

Despite all these discussions about human's quest for happiness and life satisfaction, one question remains. Does God want me to be happy? A lot of Christians think that they should share in the suffering of Christ. So they glorify poverty and misery as part of God's plan for their lives. However, there are so many Bible verses about happiness or joy. Some Bible versions use the word "happy" while others use the word "blessed." For example, "Happy is the man who findeth wisdom," (Proverbs 3:13, KJV) or "Blessed is the one who does not walk in step with the wicked…" (Psalm 1:1, NIV) Furthermore, the word "joy" or "rejoice" is presented as if it is a command and a choice to be made despite external circumstances. "Rejoice in the Lord always." (Philippians 4:4, NIV) So, does God want me to be happy? I believe so. But more than that, He wants us to have a joyful attitude under any circumstance.

One verse in the Bible sums up the Aristotelian concepts of eudaimonic and hedonic happiness. Ecclesiastes 3:12-13 (ESV) says, "I perceived that there is nothing better for them than to be joyful and to do good as long as they live; also that everyone should eat and drink and take pleasure in all his toil—this is God's gift to man." In the first part of this text, notice that it mentioned being joyful and doing good. "Doing good" to others is the exact concept for eudaimonic happiness. On the other hand, "everyone should eat and drink and take pleasure in all his toil" exactly describes what hedonic happiness is. It is about granting pleasures for the self. And doesn't the last line, "this is God's gift to man," show the heart of God desiring happiness and life satisfaction for us? He really is a good God! Some people think that being a Christ-follower will restrict us from having fun and pleasure. But remember that pleasures approved by God bring blessings without sorrows.

"I perceived that there is nothing better for them than to be joyful and to do good as long as they live; also that everyone should eat and drink and take pleasure in all his toil—this is God's gift to man."
Ecclesiastes 3:12-13 (ESV)

I Was No Longer Happy So I Quit

A year after getting my master's degree, I enrolled in a doctoral program. This was my first attempt at getting a Ph.D. It was an online program, too. However, I only lasted two years in this program and did not finish it. I earned 24 credits, was on track with my coursework, and was getting straight A's. If I had remained in the program for two more years, I would have finished my doctoral degree in 2018. But I quit. Why? Because I was no longer happy i.e. joyful in this pursuit. My life felt like a complete mess.

Before arriving at my final decision to quit the program, I was so horrified that it gave me literal chills and recurring nightmares for many sleepless, restless nights. Just the thought, that I was giving up, and never finishing what I started gave me anxiety and panic attacks. What helped me get through this season was writing in my journal.

Writing about my feelings was therapeutic and it helped me leave that chapter and close it with peace. In one writing episode, I created two columns on a piece of paper. The first one was why I should continue in my doctoral program, and the other one was why I should stop. The list in the first column was very short. I just wanted to be a Dr. like my other colleagues and I didn't want to be a *quitter*. For one working in academia, a doctorate degree is *precious*. But alas, it was such a pathetic reason to pursue a doctoral degree. I felt my stomach turning upside down with this realization.

The list in the second column, "Why I should stop," needed additional pages because they were too many. First, I was no longer happy and I felt I was being robbed of joy and inner peace. I was single, but I was not living a balanced life anymore. I could no longer find fulfillment in the assignments I was doing, and was no longer sure if there was anything beyond getting a degree other than getting more classes to teach. And this only meant more work. Bigger pay, yes. But nonetheless, more work! That meant, I would struggle to find balance in life and well-being. It was going to be a vicious cycle. That was such a depressive thought.

I knew it was getting worse when I became anxious and felt dread every time I opened my student portal. I had to take deep breaths and summon courage just to open my graded assignments and read my professor's feedback. I was maximizing my procrastination parameters and ended up submitting my papers late or not at all. Then, I started doing something out of my character. I dropped some of my courses. I had three per semester. It was hard to admit defeat but listing all these down into writing brought relief and assurance. After so much tears and prayers, I came to peace that I needed to quit the program.

Connecting the Dots

I did not only quit my doctoral program, but I also took a semester off–a sabbatical leave from work. That was how miserable I was with my life then. I traveled to Davao[7] and volunteered at an organization for a month. There I worked with other volunteers at peace-making efforts. Then, I traveled to the United States where I was invited to speak at a youth conference in Florida. I also took the time to visit my brother in North Carolina, as well as some friends in New Jersey and Michigan. Then, I went to Indonesia for a month. I met many people, and made many new friends. There was a lot of learning and spiritual growth. It was a refreshing time to recalibrate my perspectives and rejuvenate my relationship with God. The best thing that happened in this season of quitting was meeting Johnny, my husband now.

Looking back, I connected the dots. If I had not quit my doctoral program and temporarily left my job, my husband and I would never have met. I would have had no time to entertain romance, and eventually get married a year later. The month of our wedding was also the month when some of my classmates from the doctoral cohort were graduating. Since I was in a state of happiness, joy, and life satisfaction, I did not feel an ounce of envy or jealousy at them for accomplishing that academic goal. Rather, everything felt right because I knew that had I continued with my doctoral pursuit, I would have missed the love of my life.

Do Not Sacrifice Your Peace

So, for you, my dear online learner. If there is one thing you should be sure about, make certain that your happiness and life satisfaction are not put on hold. Your peace and joy should not be sacrificed at the altar of academic pursuit. The prestige you are craving for will not be satisfied with a college diploma or any higher education degree alone. There is more to life than this. You should be happy and satisfied while you are getting your degree. It is not the other way around. A degree will not bring you happiness and life satisfaction. But you should pursue your degree from a place of happiness and life satisfaction.

Happiness will ebb and flow during your academic journey. Finding a solid ground to remain in the state of joy will be up to the daily choices you make. For example, one day, you get a final grade of A in a difficult assignment. There will be bursts of happiness that will shoot through

---

7   Davao is a province in one of the southern islands in the Philippines

your nerves. Enjoy it while this feeling of happiness lasts because a few weeks later, you might find yourself deeply stuck in the next assignment of the new course you are enrolled in. You can no longer draw happiness from that grade of A on the previous course you just finished. However, you can draw the joy from deep within you by reminding yourself of the strength and resilience you gained from overcoming the challenges in the previous course.

Let's Wrap It Up!

We know that the quest for happiness and life satisfaction is deeply embedded in human history, not only based on scientific sources but also based on the Word of God. It is God's desire for us to find true happiness, joy, peace, and life satisfaction. The academic term, *hedonia,* refers to happiness based on pleasure, enjoyment, comfort, and absence from distress while *eudaimonia* refers to happiness based on growth, meaning, authenticity, and excellence. It is amazing that God's word also speaks about finding pleasure in things such as eating and drinking. Moreover, God's word also talks about being joyful in doing good and rejoicing at all times.

As an online learner, never think that a degree would bring you happiness and life satisfaction. In fact, you should be pursuing your academic goals from the position of happiness and life satisfaction, not the other way around. If you are not in this position right now, please read on and check the other parameters of human flourishing that you may need to examine within yourself. Nehemiah 8:10 is my prayer for all my students and you as the reader of this book. I pray that you will enjoy choice foods and sweet drinks. May you have so much abundance, not only of material or financial things, but also of spiritual gifts so that you can share with those who have nothing. May you never grieve but experience that the joy of the Lord is your strength.

"...Go and enjoy choice food and sweet drinks, and send some to those who have nothing prepared. This day is holy to our Lord. Do not grieve, for the joy of the Lord is your strength,"
Nehemiah 8:10 (NIV)

Chapter 5

HEALTH IS
THE NEW HUSTLE

"Dear friend, I pray that you may enjoy good health and that all may go well with you, even as your soul is getting along well." 3 John 1:2 (NIV)

"Bru, just go to the health clinic and get yourself checked," Sienna said softly. I have four colleagues that became my closest friends and *bru*, pronounced like *true*, was our pet name for each other. It's not pronounced as *bruh*, and certainly not *bro*.

I had not been feeling well over the weekend. That Sunday night, I had terrible headaches, shortness of breath, and could not sleep. So, on Monday morning, I missed my 7 AM class to sleep some more. Somewhat feeling better at noon, I came to the campus to teach the rest of my classes for the day. However, I had to catch my breath as I spoke in the class. I thought of a quick group work that students could do so I could sit down and rest. I thought maybe I was over-fatigued. After the class, I went back to the faculty room where Sienna, my friend and colleague, saw me.

I was glad I did what she suggested. She told me later that she did not like how I looked and knew something was wrong. The nurse at the clinic was shocked at how high my blood pressure was and sent me straight to the hospital. I was confined for three days, and the doctor could not figure out what was wrong with me, as my blood pressure would not go down but my bloodwork results were all fine. That was the first time I was ever confined to the hospital, and I was so scared. Even as a child, I never got sick enough to be confined. Sure, I would see the doctor, but I'd be given a prescription and sent home to recuperate.

"Can't I just go home and rest?" I asked the doctor.

"Ma'am, we can't let you go home until your blood pressure stabilizes. You could have a stroke with these numbers. Even with medications, your blood pressure is still high. We have to wait until it gets back to normal so you can manage it from home," the doctor patiently explained to me.

The Scary Combination

It was a health scare, and I had enough time to reflect while lying on the hospital bed, staring at the ceiling. Yes, I knew exactly how I got there. While I had decades of bad health habits, the past couple months were the worst. I was eating very badly: junk food, *lechon*,[8] sweets, etc. I was only sleeping four hours at most every day. And I was sedentary on my computer for more than 12 hours as I was working on a project. I would come in as early as 6:30 AM and go home around 10 PM. The only time I would be standing or walking was when I had to go to my classes. Otherwise, I was sedentary the rest of the time. Additionally, a lot was going on in my mind. The doctor asked me if I had been stressing out on something. Since my bloodwork was fine, he guessed that the problem had mental roots; he could not have been more accurate.

Anxiety!

I was closing everything in my life in the Philippines. I had projects at work that I had to finish. Then everything I owned in my apartment had to be disposed of, sold, or packed away. I was preparing for US

---

8   Lechon is a crispy, roasted pork, a popular and iconic dish in the Philippines. It's traditionally spit-roasted over an open flame, often served during celebrations and special occasions.

immigration interviews, had to get an executive medical exam with required vaccinations, attend an immigration, in-person seminar, and prepare or gather tons of documents that I needed to restart life in the US. I had to tend to my bank accounts, insurance, social security, taxes, stocks, etc. At the same time, I was thinking about how I could plan a wedding in Arizona, a place I'd never been to and knew no one except Johnny, my fiance. With about two months left, I was also thinking about how I could fit into my schedule all the circles of friends I wanted to meet for the last time and say goodbye.

My stress and anxiety were at the maximum level.

And the diagnosis of high blood pressure only increased my anxiety. My anxiety, in turn, increased my high blood pressure! What a perfect lethal combination.

Mental and Physical Health

That was a wake-up call. All the bad habits from my teenage years and in my 20s were finally catching up. I realized I was not immune to diseases and it was time to make changes. Furthermore, I had never been affected by stress and anxiety so hard that it physically manifested in high blood pressure. Taking care of mental and physical health must go in tandem. While mental health refers to a person's emotional, psychological, and social well-being, physical health is the ability to move and function with ease.

Mental and physical health are inseparable, affecting one another. If one is physically sick, having a strong mental capacity to help the body get better is scientifically proven helpful. On the other hand, there are cases where mental illnesses are cured when the physical body gets proper nourishment, enough sleep, and adequate exercise. Mental health is critical as thought patterns affect behavior, and consistent behavior becomes an identity. Then, an identity is manifested in physical health. Furthermore, functionality, productivity, and overall quality of life depend primarily on physical health. Aside from inherited genes and environmental factors, lifestyle choices and behavioral patterns impact physical and mental health.

The mental and physical health of online learners is vital to carrying out essential tasks effectively and efficiently. As society becomes more aware and accepting of mental health problems, the stigma of seeking professional medical help decreases. When I was in college, discussions about mental health were taboo. Decades later, as a professor, I get lots of messages from students sharing their mental health problems. They share about their anxiety or panic attacks, depression, and suicidal thoughts without hesitation, embarrassment, or shame. As I became more aware of the gravity of mental health problems, my sensitivity to word usage, tone, and message when communicating with students increased.

Mental Triggers

I had a student whose anger got triggered when I used the words *"blah...blah..."* in my announcements instead of *etc.* or *and so forth.* He called his counselor and withdrew from the class. The counselor reported me to my boss, and I got called out. I have used these words in my classes before and I never had a problem until this student. Another student almost failed my class because there was one week in our course where Title IX[9] was discussed and she flatly refused to do anything with it. She did not submit any of the assignments. In our private messages, she mentioned that she had traumatic experiences that triggered her anxiety whenever a discussion is related to anything sexual.

Mental triggers are powerful because they can provoke behavior and invoke feelings. If you have a behavior or feelings that you don't understand or can't control, figure out your mental triggers. For example, if you easily get angry, there is a reason behind that. What is causing your anger? No, it is not just because somebody used words like *blah...blah...* in their writing. There is a deeper reason than that. Were you dismissed, unheard, and disrespected in the past? You may need professional help from a counselor or therapist to help you unpack your trauma and triggers. This is very important because your mental state affects your overall health. Be aware of your thought patterns and where you allow your thoughts to run into. Most of the time, you have to consciously

---

9   Title IX is a federal civil rights law in the United States that prohibits sex-based discrimination in any education program or activity receiving federal funds. Title IX protects against sex-based discrimination, sexual harassment, and sexual assault in educational settings.

call out your mind to stop going towards the dark. Take every thought captive in obedience to Christ (2 Corinthians 10:5).

Health Habits

Online learners can get so busy that they often neglect their health habits. You can get too preoccupied and busy when studying. It is easy to forgo the time used for physical exercise and use it for studying instead. Sitting too long in front of your computer can lead to a sedentary and unhealthy lifestyle. Preparing and cooking your own meals requires energy and time, and I guess you can use that time for studying instead. While you do your homework, getting into the habit of eating unhealthy snacks, such as crunchy chips, or drinking sugary beverages can eventually have detrimental repercussions. Staying up late at night to do homework and not getting enough sleep can become the normal routine. Routines become a habit.

A habit frequently repeated becomes a lifestyle.

Physical movements. Being sedentary such as sitting too long in front of the computer to do homework could go unnoticed. If your work requires you to sit at your work desk for more or less than 8 hours a day, plus several more hours at night to do academic work, then this is not healthy. Since there is nothing you can do right now to change this situation, you need to incorporate creative strategies to give yourself an opportunity to move. For example, you can park your car at the farthest parking spot so you can walk more. You can take the stairs instead of the elevator. Go up and down several flights of stairs for five to ten minutes during your lunch break. If you are working from home like me, you can also do some squats, sit-ups, or push-ups every two to three hours.

Honestly, I failed to take care of my physical health. After decades of bad sedentary habits, my physique is not what it used to be. I used to lose a lot of weight faster with just a few skipped meals, and minimum exercise. Due to age and hormones, it is a challenge to get back into good physical shape. I wish somebody would have reminded me ten years ago to incorporate lots of movements in my daily routines. If you are like me, please do not give up hope. We have to keep trying and never give up!

After getting my Ph.D., I was determined to include physical movements as part of my lifestyle. I started taking barre classes, joined a hiking group, and incorporated some movements into my daily routines. Many years of using the computer made my wrists weak (which could lead to carpal tunnel) and I could tell I was starting to lose muscle mass in my legs and arms. So, my primary goal for this lifestyle change was to get stronger first. Although I still need to do a lot of work to get into the best shape, I feel that I am regaining more strength and flexibility.

If you are also struggling to incorporate active, physical movements into your lifestyle as an online student, put it in the schedule. It can be 10 minutes, 20 minutes, or one hour of exercise in your day. It doesn't have to be every day, either. Three to four times a week is better than nothing. Consider each physical movement that you intentionally do as a vote for your future healthy self. You don't have to have a perfect streak of daily exercise. You just need the majority of the days in a week to be moving and exercising.

Adequate sleep. Lack of sleep can lead to diseases such as high blood pressure, diabetes, obesity, depression, and heart attack. Remember, prevention is better than cure. As an online student, I know it is hard to get eight hours of sleep. But you can function so much better if you have a good sleep. You would be more alert, more focused, more energetic, and generally would be in a better mood. Just like physical movements, it is understandable if there are nights that you cannot go to sleep early because of an assignment. That is OK. Remember, majority wins the vote, not perfection. Find pockets of time within the day to do small academic tasks so you don't have to do them all at night. For example, if you have an hour lunch break, use 30 minutes of that break for doing one small academic task. It could be as simple as reading one of the assigned journal resources for your major assignment. You can finish that in 30 minutes.

I had a terrible sleep habit for many years. But I aim to get better at it. I quit drinking caffeine after 2 PM. If I feel like getting coffee in the afternoon, I take decaf. Before, coffee was my dessert after dinner. I never tracked my hours of sleep before, but now I do. I am getting better at winding down and being in bed by 9 PM, but I still struggle to get a straight eight hours of sleep. Sometimes, I would wake up in the middle of the night with an alert mind, and find it difficult to go back to sleep. However, since I became more conscious of my sleep habits, I have made significant progress.

When I get my 8 hours of sleep, there is no brain fog. I feel energetic throughout the day, and I am more focused and in a good mood all day long. I don't have an afternoon crash that calls for a nap. I realized that when I was a student, I could have worked around my schedule and studied earlier in the day instead of starting at 9 PM and studying until midnight. It really is a matter of priority and organization of things in the schedule. I admit that sleep was never a priority for me before!

Nutrition. Physical movements and adequate sleep must be paired with good nutrition. As an online student, it is so easy to fall into bad eating habits. It is so much easier to buy fast food or takeout instead of cooking a healthier meal, especially if you have picky children to feed. I don't judge you for that. It is so hard to cook because cooking comes with the additional tasks of grocery shopping, food storage, and cleaning the kitchen which could take two hours of your night. It is easier to do takeout or have microwaveable dinners. Coffee, crunchy snacks such as chips, or sweets like chocolates provide comfort for the lonely nights when you are studying by yourself, fighting sleepiness and boredom while the rest of the household sleeps.

But then again, it is a matter of priority. You make time for what matters to you. You figure out what works best for you. You can make grocery shopping and meal preparations as a weekend thing. Then, you can cook two to three dishes in big batches and reheat them throughout the week. Instead of snacking on chips, try snacking on crunchy vegetables such as carrots, celery, and bell peppers. The sound of the crunch can do the same task of keeping you awake as much as what oily and salty chips with empty calories can. If good nutrition is part of your goal so you can flourish more in physical health and mental spaces, then no excuses should be allowed.

I am writing about this because I have failed in this area, and if I could turn back time, I would make better choices. But now that it is in the past, I will keep moving forward. Part of that is telling online students to make better choices when it comes to incorporating physical movements, getting adequate sleep, and committing to healthier nutrition. Remember, it is all about your small but consistent choices every day that make up your life.

Connection of Physical and Mental Health

The Bible has interesting perspectives about mental and physical health. First, "Do you not know that your bodies are temples of the Holy Spirit, who is in you, whom you have received from God? You are not your own; you were bought at a price. Therefore, honor God with your bodies." (1 Corinthians 6:19-20, NIV) If we consider our physical bodies the way this verse teaches us, that they are temples of the Holy Spirit, then we will take care of them in a way that honors God.

What are some ways we can take care of our physical or mental health? "Do not be wise in your own eyes; fear the Lord and shun evil. This will bring health to your body and nourishment to your bones." (Proverbs 3:7-8,NIV) Then, you should "...be not conformed to this world, but be ye transformed by the renewing of your mind, that ye may prove what is that good, and acceptable, and perfect, will of God." (Romans 12:2, KJV) If our renewed minds can discern the good, acceptable, and perfect will of God and obey Him, then we can be spared from so many heartaches and problems, right?

How Do We Renew Our Minds?

There are two ways we can renew our minds: meditation and prayers.

The world raves about the benefits of meditation, but it takes God out of the equation. Read the comforting passage of Psalms, filled with wisdom and inspiration. There you will see how King David's meditation was all about connecting with God. "I remember the days of long ago; I meditate on all your works and consider what your hands have done." (Psalm 143:5, NIV)

Praying does wonders for our minds, too. "Do not be anxious about anything, but in every situation, by prayer and petition, with thanksgiving, present your requests to God. And the peace of God, which transcends all understanding, will guard your hearts and your minds in Christ Jesus." (Philippians 4:6-7, NIV)

Check your thought patterns and keep discerning the will of God–good, acceptable, and perfect. If these three characteristics are absent, then we know it is not God's will for us, and we can reject those in our minds. Philippians 4:8 also describes the things that our minds should dwell on. These are things that are true, honorable, just, pure, lovely, commendable, excellent, and anything worthy of praise!

Routines and Schedules

You can do many small things for yourself each day to promote mental and physical health. Choose one health habit at a time and keep stacking it up until those habits become a lifestyle. Stacking good habits means you are adding one good habit to the one you already established. Establish a routine in your day and a schedule in your week. Remember, small habits accumulated through the years become your lifestyle. Routines and schedules provide stability. It does not mean you are not flexible and open to changes in your day. It just means that you know exactly what to get back to after a disruption. This lessens stress and anxiety!

About two years ago, I established a morning routine. Because of these routines, I became more consistent and better at getting morning exercise. I set the alarm at 4:50 AM, get up at 5:00 AM, leave the house at 5:10 AM, and get to the barre studio in time for my 5:30 AM exercise. Then, I get back home at 6:40 AM, get showered, dressed up, and ready for the day! I clean and tidy up the house in the morning, then I make coffee and have my morning devotions. Drinking coffee and reading the Bible is a good pair and can be done in 10-15 minutes. Before I established my morning routines and weekly schedules, I had terrible habits of working in my pajamas, sleeping in, and not taking a shower before I started my day. I used to only read my Bible when I felt like it, and cleaned our house once it got unbearably messy. But for the past two years since I implemented this morning routine, my physical and mental health improved!

Practical Tip for Online Learners

Establish your routines with good habits. These good habits accumulate and they become your identity, your lifestyle. If you write a to-do list for your daily tasks, make a to-do list of habits for your mental and physical health. This will give you an overview of the habits you must work on to acquire and become part of your daily lifestyle. Some examples of healthy habits you can include on your to-do health list may consist of the time to wake up, step on the scale and record your weight, exercise, take vitamins, proper diet, meditation or daily devotions, prayer time, and time to sleep.

Write these vertically, and then write the dates for the week horizontally on the top of the page. Every day, under the date, write a check next to the healthy habits you have gifted yourself. It is OK not to have a perfect track record. You only need the majority of the days in each week, remember? So, at the end of each week, make sure you give yourself a majority of votes for good choices pertaining to your mental and physical health.

Let's Wrap It Up!

Engaging in healthy behaviors, such as exercising regularly, eating a healthy diet, getting enough sleep, managing stress, and seeking support from friends, family, or mental and physical health professionals, improves overall well-being. Good mental health can help you cope with stress and challenges, and maintain a positive outlook in life. On the other hand, good physical health can help you engage in physical activities, reducing the risk of chronic diseases. Also, do not forget to look into God's Word and meditate on it. Praying does wonders for mental health as it can uplift burdens and worries. Take good care of your mental and physical health to keep flourishing!

Chapter 6

LIVE WHAT YOU BELIEVE

> *"...add to your faith virtue; and to virtue knowledge; and to knowledge temperance; and to temperance patience; and to patience godliness; and to godliness brotherly kindness; and to brotherly kindness charity..."*
> *2 Peter 1:5-8 (KJV)*

Your character, virtues, and values must be aligned with your degree and profession. Misalignment will keep you from flourishing. If you are compassionate, patient, and kind, a nursing or teaching degree might suit you. If you have lots of courage, bravery, and a strong sense of justice, a law or justice degree can be your future career. If you are curious, expressive, and sensitive to the needs of others, a profession in the arts or humanities can be your calling. If you are creative, competitive, and outgoing, then building a business can be your future.

One of the advantages of being an adult when you pursue an online degree is that your brain has been fully developed and your life experiences have already taught you what you're good at. You already know your strengths and weaknesses, and probably the reason why you're pursuing a degree online is because you already know what you want. Most importantly, you are already aware of most of your character traits, virtues, and values. Be thankful that you have this advantage over

18-year-olds whose developing brains are still figuring it out. However, even as adults, we should reflect on where the strength of our character, virtues, and values lie and whether they are aligned with our pursuits in life.

Deep Desires versus a Career

I have former students who are not flourishing because their character, virtues, and values are not aligned with their profession. On the other hand, there are also some who are in a profession that is so different from the degree they got. But they are flourishing because their work is aligned to their character, virtues, and values.

I was at an airport lounge in Manila, waiting for my flight to board for South Korea, when I heard somebody shouting my name. I turned around and saw Grace, my former student. She graduated as a chemical engineer, got her license, and snagged a competitive job right away. I had her in several of the courses I taught, and I was the editor of her thesis before she graduated. Through the years on campus, she would always stop and chat with me whenever our paths crossed. Sometimes, she would come to my office for a casual chat and share life updates.

It had been several years since she graduated, and I was glad she remembered me. We were on the same flight, but my trip was for a vacation while hers was for a business meeting. We spent the next few hours talking during our flight. She worked as a chemical engineer, but was unhappy and dissatisfied with life. She said that her only consolation was the fat paycheck and benefits from the company, but she hated the long hours, extensive travels, and constant danger of getting accidentally exposed to chemicals in the laboratory. She developed allergies and a lung condition that made her extra sensitive to the slightest exposure. These were taking a toll on her health, making her anxious and dissatisfied with life.

It was hard to talk to someone who knows that their values no longer align with their career and yet, they won't leave it due to the financial security it provides. She was lost, confused, and didn't know what to do.

"People envy my job because I travel to different countries. But they don't know that I only go from the airport to the hotel, get my job done, then go back home. I don't even have time for sightseeing as most tourists do!"

She told me she wanted to have more free time so she could spend it with her family or friends, attend social events, go on dates, and eventually get married and have her own family, too.

"But how can I?" she said. "Most of my waking hours are spent at work! I go to work before the sun is up and get home at almost midnight! I have no time to even go on dates, so how can I sustain a relationship?" Tears were welling in her eyes, and I gave her a hug.

Softly and tenderly, I told her frankly that her career was not aligned to what her heart was yearning for. At that moment, what she valued was financial security. But deep in her heart, she had desires that were not aligned to her current choices. She was shocked at what I said and was in denial for a bit.

"Yes, dear," I insisted. "Money is your priority right now. You value it more than those deep desires in your heart. If your fat paycheck and benefits are taken away, you will leave that job, right?" Eventually, before our flight arrived in Seoul, she seemed enlightened about the misalignment of her deep desires versus her career. We parted ways, and I never heard from her again. I hope she's no longer lost and confused.

Unfortunately, there are many people like Grace that hate their job and only stay due to financial security. This can be dangerous because it can affect positive character traits and highly esteemed virtues. Grace used to be outgoing, adventurous, fun-spirited, and carefree. But when I saw her at the airport, these qualities were gone. She was hopeless, and with her negative outlook on her situation, she felt doomed.

Search for What You Value Most

April experienced once how it was like to flourish in her career. She has a very pleasant and warm personality. She was a flight attendant and she loved her job when she was still single. It was aligned with her degree in hospitality management. She was flourishing and loved leading the flight crew in giving excellent service to travelers. After ten years in her career, she got married and started a family. Soon after, she gave birth to her firstborn son, but returned to full-time work after her maternity leave. That was when feelings of discontent started. She struggled with her emotions every time she had to leave the baby. Long-haul flights across the globe meant being gone for several days. She got a break for a day or two and had to do it all over again. She began hating her job.

After two years, a baby girl joined the family. This time, it became harder to return to work and depression set in. She cried in despair and finally shared her struggles with her husband. After spending so much time in reflection, prayer, and seeking counseling from other couples in their church, she decided to leave her career. It was a big sacrifice. She still loved what she did, but she couldn't bear being away too much from her children. She needed the job for financial reasons, but it did not align with what she valued most–time with her family.

I met April in my masters' cohort. Even though our program was online, my classmates and I made an effort to meet in person for dinner. April and I connected well and became fast friends. She had already left her career and decided to get a master's degree so she could teach in college. She was currently working as a part-time instructor to hospitality management students. Sure, she missed the fat paycheck, but she was very happy that she had more time to be with her husband and children.

Grace and April both struggled to flourish when there was a misalignment between their careers and their values. This misalignment caused friction in their character and virtues, highly impacting their lives. As I mentioned before, you don't have to wait for life to happen to you before you reflect. You can look at other people's lives and reflect on theirs because, "ye shall know them by their fruits." (Matthew 7:16, KJV) Search for what you value most. Examine your character and virtues. If these go into friction with your career, you need to reassess your life and determine how to align them. Don't think that your situation is hopeless. Get out of that victim mentality and stop acting helpless.

My Pivot Story

My college degree is in elementary education. I just turned 20 when I started teaching at a Christian elementary school. I loved the fifth-graders I taught, as they brought me so much joy. I am sure I have the virtues of patience, kindness, and compassion for children perfectly suited for an elementary teacher. But college did not prepare me to deal with the parents and exude the same virtues of patience, kindness, and compassion at their demands. I love all the children in my classes (well, maybe except for a few unforgettable ones) and I had such fond memories of humor and anecdotes that happened every day in my class.

However, dealing with the parents when it comes to disciplining their children, or mediating between parents who argued over their fighting children was beyond my capacity. When students fought on the playground, or one got bruised after recess, I became nervous and anxious about their parents coming in for an explanation. When students forgot an assignment and I gave them zero, the parents would come the next day and ask me why. When a student felt left out from cliques, the parents would come marching in demanding that I not allow cliques and that I made sure nobody was left out during recess.

One parent gave me parenting books, and remarked, "I know you're too young to understand me because you're not a parent yet."

One time, I had a terrible encounter with a helicopter parent. After she left, I just collapsed in my chair and cried and cried. The school principal and another colleague silently consoled me. I came home with bloodshot eyes and a puffy face that alarmed my mother. That was when I knew that teaching at the elementary level was not for me.

So, when an opportunity came to join an international exchange program, I grabbed it. I dabbled some more in elementary, middle school, and high school levels as I helped teachers at Shalom Christian Academy in Pennsylvania during my assignment as a volunteer. When I came back to the Philippines after a year, I was unsure what to do with my life and career, but I knew I could not go back to full-time elementary teaching. I taught English as a Second Language to Koreans for 16 months before I had the courage to apply as an English instructor in a newly established, small college. Thus, my career in higher education began. At present, I teach doctoral students, too.

My kindness, patience, and compassion are still tested sometimes. But pivoting my teaching career at the higher levels of education meant no interference from parents, and it lessened my stress and anxiety.

Looking back, I realized that my decision to pivot my career was because I also value peace of mind.

The Interplay of Character, Virtues, and Values

Can you see how character, virtues, and values are interrelated? These three are elements of a person's moral identity; hence, they are essential in human flourishing. Nature, nurture, and life experiences shape these qualities and characteristics. They include things like honesty, responsibility, kindness, and self-control. On the other hand, virtue refers to moral excellence and righteous behavior, the habit of choosing to do the right thing even when it is difficult or unpopular. Virtues are seen as desirable qualities because they help promote the well-being of the individual and society. The character of a person is known through observable traits in their actions. Yet, these are anchored within the virtues they hold fast to in the deepest chambers of their hearts. Values, however, are things people prioritize and give importance to. Character, virtues, and values subtly play a role in human flourishing, aptly supported by Biblical principles, and can be significantly strengthened through conscious efforts.

Character, virtues, and values have been the subject of philosophical inquiry for thousands of years as they seem to be linked to happiness, justice, and the good life. Even today, psychologists, sociologists, and educators are all looking for ways in which these can be developed, cultivated, and integrated or taught through education, role modeling, and intentional efforts. Online students with positive character traits, such as honesty, compassion, self-control, discipline, and courage, tend to experience higher life satisfaction and well-being. Likewise, those whose guiding virtues provide a moral framework for decision-making lead more fulfilling lives. Going back to April's story, you will notice that she was able to navigate her challenging situation and make a decision that aligned with her values. After deciding to leave her flight attendant career, she found a deeper sense of purpose and meaning in life.

I was once a faculty chair, and I supervised around 20 faculty members. I also sat in interviews and teaching demonstrations during the hiring process. I was also responsible for training new hires. One of my frustrations was new hires leaving after a semester because this meant

I would have to go through the whole hiring process again. During exit interviews, when asked why they were leaving, most would say that they found new opportunities. But there are some faculty who would admit that there were workplace policies that clashed with their character, virtues, and values.

For example, one of the faculty I supervised left because he was deeply bothered that the school did not allow fraternities for students and a labor union for employees. These were clearly forbidden in the workplace policy, and clearly discussed during the hiring process. Another faculty resigned because she did not like the teaching schedule because the courses she taught were in the evenings or on Saturdays. She wanted those hours and weekends to be spent with family instead. In recent years, you have also probably heard of some military personnel resigning from their posts because of the mandatory COVID-19 vaccination. These are just some examples of situations where one's virtue does not align with a company's virtues or policies. Time and circumstances reveal and test the character, virtues, and values we hold dear.

Principles from the Scriptures

Scripture is full of caution about character and virtues that are guiding principles toward a flourishing life. For example, Colossians 3:12-14 (NIV) says, "Therefore, as God's chosen people, holy and dearly loved, clothe yourselves with compassion, kindness, humility, gentleness, and patience. Bear with each other and forgive one another if any of you has a grievance against someone. Forgive as the Lord forgave you. And over all these virtues put on love, which binds them all together in perfect unity."

It is not common to hear or read about forgiveness being a virtue. Still, psychologists would agree that many troubled people are those who choose not to forgive. In the last line of this verse, notice how it says that love binds beautiful character and virtue together. Interestingly, the Bible hints that possessing good character and virtue is not only for the benefit of other people, but ultimately, it is a benefit for the person who exhibits it. "Those who are kind benefit themselves, but the cruel bring ruin on themselves." (Proverbs 11:17, NIV) You benefit from living with godly character and virtues!

God's power has granted us all things that pertain to life and godliness with many precious and great promises so that we can escape the corruption in this world. Because of this God-given power, we can add to our faith some virtues, then to virtues some knowledge, then self-control, steadfastness, godliness, affection, love, and "...if you possess these qualities in increasing measure, they will keep you from being ineffective and unproductive...." (2 Peter 1:8, NIV) Character and virtue will keep us from being ineffective and unfruitful! This verse summarized what researchers and experts are trying to point out about the significance of character and virtue in human flourishing!

So, What Are in These for You?

Character, virtues, and values play a fundamental role in the lives of online learners. Unlike traditional students, adult learners often juggle multiple responsibilities, such as work, family, and financial obligations alongside their studies. Key virtues like perseverance, discipline, and resilience help you stay committed to your educational journey despite challenges. You need to persevere to continue your studies even when faced with difficulties. Meanwhile, discipline allows you to manage time effectively and balance academic tasks with personal and professional responsibilities. These virtues will enable you to stay focused on your goals and overcome obstacles with determination.

Integrity and responsibility are also crucial virtues that guide adult learners in their academic journey. Online learning requires a high level of self-motivation and ethical behavior, as there is no direct supervision from professors. Upholding academic honesty, meeting deadlines, and maintaining a strong work ethic demonstrates integrity, which fosters credibility and personal growth. Responsibility, on the other hand, will help you stay accountable in your progress, ensuring you complete coursework on time and actively participate in your education. By embodying these virtues, you, as an online learner, can set a positive example for your peers, family, and colleagues, reinforcing the importance of lifelong learning.

Ultimately, character and virtues shape the overall success and personal development of online learners. A strong moral compass, coupled with virtues like perseverance, integrity, and responsibility, will help you navigate the challenges of online education while maintaining balance in other areas of your life. These traits not only contribute to academic achievement but also enhance your personal and professional growth. By cultivating strong character and virtues, online learners develop the resilience and discipline needed to thrive in both studies and future endeavors.

Let's Wrap It Up!

Character, virtues, and values are critical components of human flourishing. By developing these qualities, you can experience higher levels of well-being, and contribute to the well-being of society as a whole. When you possess positive character traits and virtues, you are more likely to engage in prosocial behavior and contribute to the common good. This helps build stronger communities and promotes a more just and equitable society. Contemporary research findings and the Bible's teachings agree that character, virtues, and values play a critical role in shaping our lives and the lives of those around us. By developing and nurturing these qualities, we can live more fulfilling lives and positively impact the world.

Chapter 7

CHASING PURPOSE, NOT PERFECTION

"I am crucified with Christ: nevertheless I live; yet not I, but Christ liveth in me: and the life which I now live in the flesh, I live by the faith of the Son of God, who loved me, and gave himself for me." Galatians 2:20 (KJV)

Finally, after a grueling year of writing the first three chapters of my dissertation, which was the proposal, I submitted it to my dissertation committee for review. This was a great milestone, and I was so relieved and happy. But, suddenly I had nothing to do! I did not realize how writing a dissertation took a lot of my time. Now, I was doing nothing and it was only in the middle of the day. I was done with my job-related work and all the household chores. This was the time I used to spend writing. The relief and happiness dissipated as panic gripped my heart. I wondered if I was missing something that I should be doing. Then, it dawned on me, "What am I going to do after I'm done with my Ph.D.?" This sneak peek of life after Ph.D. gave me a gnawing sense of fear to the unknown and uncharted territory. All my life, studying has brought me a sense of meaning and purpose (read my detailed account at the end of the chapter, "Before the Book"). Now that I reached the pinnacle of higher education, what's next?

As a learner, studying gave me meaning and purpose in my life. It gave me direction and motivation, providing a foundation for decision-making and goal-setting. After high school, I wanted to go to college so that I could find a good job. After finding a job, I wanted to pursue a master's degree to get job tenure and a higher pay. After my master's, I wanted a Ph.D. to flourish in my higher education career. Now that I almost had my Ph.D. within reach, I realized I was already flourishing in my college teaching career, and getting a Ph.D. wouldn't change it very much (or so I thought at the time). So, now what? Was there something for me beyond teaching online in college?

Finding meaning and having a purpose in life while I was studying gave me a sense of identity, a reason for being, a feeling of belongingness, and assurance that things were larger than life. Studying helped me cope better with life's challenges and navigate difficulties with more grace because the meaning and purpose behind it provided a framework to make sense of difficult experiences. I trusted the process and enjoyed life's journey knowing that things would work out well. And now that formal studying had almost come to an end, I realized that I needed to find new meaning and purpose in my life to make sense out of all the education I'd achieved.

What's with Having a Sense of Meaning and Purpose?

Having a sense of meaning and purpose impacts your overall level of flourishing because it can improve your mental health, motivate you to stay in better physical shape, increase your feelings of life satisfaction, improve your cognitive function, nourish your social relationships, create a sense of identity, and increase your productivity. When you have a clear sense of purpose, you are more likely to engage in prosocial behavior and contribute to the common good, increasing your flourishing level and impacting society as a whole.

I vividly remember that day when it dawned on me that after getting my Ph.D., my life would have no more sense of meaning and purpose. I was sitting on our living room couch, absent-mindedly flipping through Netflix movies as tears rolled down my cheeks uncontrollably. But the Holy Spirit is the Comforter. Life with God taught me that an ending to something is the beginning of something new. I knew it was time to seek the Lord again and ask Him, "What's next?" I turned off the TV and went to my office. I locked the door and for the next hour, I cried and prayed and flipped through my Bible looking for a Word, a sign—a hope for the future.

Having a sense of meaning and purpose in life can be explained through psychological, philosophical, sociological, cultural, and neuroscientific perspectives. Meaning in life is essential for well-being and is found through work, relationships, and suffering. Purpose is tied to autonomy, competence, and relatedness. Meaning is enhanced when you have control over your actions and can contribute to something larger than yourself. A strong sense of purpose is linked to mental and physical health, resilience, and life satisfaction. Meaning is not inherent; you must create or realize your own purpose. You can define your own meaning through the choices you make. Purpose is often derived from social roles, cultural values, and narratives. Religion, family, and community contribute to a sense of meaning. Furthermore, meaning and purpose are linked to positive emotions.

Consequently, this can result in stronger communities promoting justice in a more equitable society. Having a sense of meaning in your life can provide you with a sense of fulfillment, a feeling of being connected to something greater than yourself, and a sense of contributing to the world in a meaningful way. On the other hand, finding purpose is the driving force behind your actions and decisions, providing a sense of direction and motivation. It can help you focus your efforts, prioritize your goals, and make sense of the challenges you face.

I Thought It Was a Concert

At that hour I was crying, praying, and seeking the Lord; I did not find answers. But an unspeakable peace transcended my soul. God has been faithful all my life, and I knew even then that He had a plan for me. After a few days, I was scrolling on social media and saw an advertisement about an event in Phoenix. It featured famous personalities and a popular gospel singer; I thought it was a concert. The ticket was very cheap, so I signed up and bought one. Then, I told my other friends about it, hoping to organize a girls' day out of it. Disappointedly, nobody said yes, and even my husband did not want to go. However, I strongly felt that I should be there. So after a few weeks, I found myself sitting alone amidst the crowd of strangers. After several worship songs, a speaker came out on the stage. Then another, and another. That's when I realized I was not at a concert. It was a Christian motivational event to inspire and teach people how to surge in life God's way.

The teachings of the Bible about finding meaning and having a purpose in life are centered on having a relationship with God and a commitment to living in accordance with His Word. The best person to ask for an explanation about an invention, its purpose, and its function, is the inventor.[10] Likewise, no one else can best show the meaning and purpose of life than the Creator Himself! That Christian event opened my eyes to the many possibilities where God could take me with life after my Ph.D. and one of them was to write this book!

Eat the Grass!

One of the teachings in that event was Psalm 23 and how God leads us into green pastures. God's green pasture is large. He leads us there, but it is our job to eat the grass! This means that all we need to do is indulge in what God places in front of us. Of course, we know that something is from God if we know Him and His character. The best way to know God's heart is to read His Word and get a glimpse of His mind. Whatever you do, work at it with all your heart as if you are working for the Lord and not for a human boss (Colossians 3:23-24). Start with what God placed in front of you and work at it faithfully. Trust God with all your heart and do not lean on your own understanding because if you submit to Him, He will make your paths straight (Proverbs 3:5-6). Sometimes, we cannot see beyond the bend in our horizon, and our logic says it does not make sense to keep going. But we need to trust God that He will be there when we reach the bend.

Seek God and His Kingdom first, and everything else will be added unto you (Matthew 6:33). All your godly pursuits, including your academic goals will be added to you, but make sure that God is the central priority in your life. There were times I was tempted to stay home on Sundays instead of going to church so that I could work on an

---

10   Warren, Rick. *The Purpose Driven Life: What on Earth Am I Here For?* Zondervan, 2002.

academic paper instead. "God understands," was my mind's defense. I was sure God would not unlove me if I chose writing academic papers on Sundays over going to church. Later, I would finish my paper, but something felt lacking. However, when I choose to go to church first, guess what happens? I still finished my paper, but this time, I felt joy and peace.

I wondered what could have happened had I not attended this Christian event. I shuddered at the thought that I would probably still be teaching the same courses I had been teaching for years. Dissatisfied and bored. But God's Word assures us that He has a great plan for our lives (Jeremiah 29:11), He has called us with a purpose (Romans 8:28), and He will make everything beautiful in His time (Ecclesiastes 3:11). The Christian event talked about real estate, stock market, income, and influence. I drank the information thirstily and digested it hungrily. I was enlightened at the great pasture of possibilities.

We are created for God's glory (Isaiah 43:7), to love and serve Him (Ecclesiastes 12:13, Matthew 22:37-39), and to share the Gospel with others (Matthew 28:19-20). How do I flourish in these areas? How can I expand my reach to share God's Word with others? These were burning questions in my mind. I cannot eat all the grass in God's great, green pasture. But what's in front of me? What can I do with what I have now? I don't have money (yet) to invest in real estate and stocks. But at the income and the influence sessions, my lifelong dream of writing a book came back to life. The glowing embers of that dying dream were reignited. Prior to this book, I have already published journal articles. In the Philippines, I have published two academic textbooks used in schools and colleges all over the country. Although these publications made me happy and accomplished to be able to call myself a published author, I knew deep in my heart that those were not the books I dreamt of writing.

For years, I was on the email list of hope*writers. I came across this community while I was still in the Philippines. While the sessions were ongoing, I thought about hope*writers because their recent emails were inviting writers to publish books with them through their publishing division, hope*books. It's no longer just a community of writers. This time, they can help you publish! These thoughts were running in my head, when suddenly, the speaker flashed the picture of Brian Dixon, owner of hope*writers! The speaker talked a little bit about Brian Dixon as one of his examples and moved on to the next slide! But I was in total shock. I was just thinking about their invitation to publish with them, and here the speaker flashed a slide about this company! If that was not a very clear and loud God-moment speaking to me, with the Holy Spirit leading the way, I don't know what it was!

I stepped out of those sessions with renewed purpose and energy. That was an affirmation that Brian Dixon and the hope*writers community were not a fraud (I have always been skeptical of anything offered online). That was a signpost, a confirmation that God was showing and leading me which way to go. I was dreading the thought of a meaningless life after getting my Ph.D. But after that, I saw the green grass around me and started eating it. I did not wait for my Ph.D. graduation to start this book. Right away, I signed up for hope*books' May 2023 cohort. I was at the thick of my proposal defense, data gathering, and data analysis, but every week, I would spend an hour in our sessions learning about publishing a book.

Ask God for Wisdom

If you still haven't found meaning in your life or if you still don't know your purpose, ask God for wisdom who gives it generously. Ask with faith and in faith, nothing wavering (James 1:5-6). God's Word contains a lot of gems you can mine to find the meaning and purpose of your life. Remember that time I was flipping absent-mindedly through Netflix movies after realizing that I may not have a purpose after my Ph.D. graduation? That was not the first time I cried and asked for God's wisdom.

Back in the day when I was discontent in my elementary teaching days, I remember going to school in the morning, dragging my feet. At the end of the long day, I would heave a big, weary sigh and look out the window. I would stare at the green mango trees and manicured lawn. Then, looking up at the vast blue sky, I would whisper, "God, is there more to life than this?" I strongly felt that God had more in store for me than my routine then. So with boldness, I declared just as Jabez prayed, "...Oh, that you would bless me and enlarge my territory..." (1

Chronicles 4:10, NIV) At every significant juncture in my life and to this day, I would boldly declare this prayer!

Think about your passions and interests. What do you like doing that you are most happy about? Make a difference in this world by putting yourself out there and trying new things, even if they are beyond your comfort zone. You will never know what you are capable of doing unless you get out of your box. Talk to your church leader, friends, families, or acquaintances and get feedback on what they think you are or will be good at.

Ask yourself what your beliefs are, what you value most, what you want to be identified and known for, and what your utmost goals and desires are. If there is one significant contribution you would like to give to humanity in this lifetime, what would it be? Work hard for it and make it your life's mission to achieve. Finding meaning and knowing your purpose may take time through reflections, prayers, journaling, and lots of waiting.

Let's Wrap It Up!

A sense of meaning and purpose is essential for human flourishing, especially for online learners, who must navigate self-directed education. Having a clear purpose provides motivation, direction, and a foundation for decision-making and goal-setting. Finding meaning and purpose in life will give you a sense of identity, belonging, and resilience in the face of challenges. By trusting the process and understanding that life's journey has a greater purpose, you can approach difficulties with grace. God's Word emphasizes that purpose is found in a relationship with God and living according to His will. The Scriptures encourage trust, service, and faith in divine plans. On a practical level, you can explore your passions, seek feedback from mentors, and step outside of your comfort zone to discover your strengths. Journaling, prayer, and self-reflection can also help you uncover a deeper sense of purpose. By aligning your actions with your values and goals, you can create a meaningful life and contribute positively to the world.

Chapter 8

FIND YOUR PEOPLE, FUEL YOUR LIFE

> *"Not giving up meeting together, as some are in the habit of doing, but encouraging one another—and all the more as you see the Day approaching," Hebrews 10:25 (NIV)*

My life is like a long bus ride. At every bus stop, some people will get out, and some will get in. Some, like my parents and siblings, have been on this bus ride with me since the beginning of my life's journey. Some people, like my best friend in first grade with whom I made a naive promise of *"friends forever,"* stayed for only a year. While some, like my friends from MCL[11] who I thought would stay forever, were left behind when my *bus* grew wings and flew to America in 2018. Such is life, I realized. We never know when people will come and go in our life. So, is it worth it to build close social relationships?

Close social relationships of good quality are integral to human life and are associated with human flourishing. People with high levels of

---

11   Malayan Colleges Laguna, now called Mapua University, was the college I worked at for 11.5 years before moving to Arizona.

flourishing often have good close social relationships. These relationships provide support, a haven of safety, and a sense of belongingness for one to thrive. People who are in good, close, social relationships also thrive in happiness and life satisfaction; mental and physical health; character, virtue, and values; meaning and purpose; and even in financial and material stability. So, the answer is yes, close social relationships are so worth it. Hence, never get tired of building and rebuilding them wherever your bus takes you and whenever new people come in at each bus stop!

Close social relationships contribute to human flourishing when physical, emotional, and spiritual support is mutually shared. Even as an online learner, I yearned for connection with my peers. My online learning experiences, both for my master's and Ph.D., were richer because of the friends I made. I could not imagine how I would have made it if not for the connection and support of my peers during those challenging milestones. Even our group chats became a safe haven to let study-related stressful things out in a rant.

One of my bus stops brought in other Ph.D. learners from my first residency. We connected well and stayed in touch through our WhatsApp group chat. Then came the part when we were in the thick of the dissertation process. I shared feelings and emotions, sometimes ranting in rage and despair. I felt validated and relieved when they jumped in and affirmed that my experiences were not unique–that they were also going through the same thing, or even worse. I also tried to share the same things to my husband, family, or friends, but pretty soon, I realized that I could not get the same compassion and understanding from them.

Make Friends with Other Online Learners

You need to find other online learners and build relationships with them. I emphasize this again in Chapter 9 with a section about how support groups are part of cultivating a healthy mindset. This is further expanded in Chapter 19, where I discuss professional relationships. It is not right for you to expect your spouse, family, or other friends to fully understand and offer the right advice for the difficult experiences you are going through as an online learner. That is unfair. Only other online learners can fully understand and offer the words you long for or need to hear. These are the only people that can truly understand you without judgment.

Lea complained to me that since she started her online class, her husband became resentful. After listening to her marital woes over the phone, I knew what to tell her. "Lea, you're not alone!" Over the years, I had students that went through the same thing. They entered a whole new world of online education, but they expect people around them to feel and see the same things only they were experiencing. Imagine it like this. You are on tour at an art museum. You decided to have a conference call with your spouse, family, and friends so that you can tell them what is going on as you walk through each gallery. You can describe what you see and what you feel. Sure, they may be listening at the other end of the line, but they are not seeing, feeling, and experiencing the art the same way you are. Do you know who does, though? Other people on that gallery tour with you! So, drop that call. Don't bother your spouse, family, and friends. Start talking to other people on that tour and perhaps you can make new friends.

I asked Lea when her husband gets resentful. "Mostly it is when I start talking about school. I shared with him what I needed to do for this course. I talked to him about the discussions in our forums. He doesn't say anything at all. He just grunts and walks away dismissively. When I tell him to take care of the kids because I have to study, he would come up with excuses such as being tired himself, or that he has something else to do…"

"Lea," I interrupted, "what do you and your husband usually enjoy talking about?"

"Oh," she paused and thought for a moment. "We love to talk about the kids, families, and politics."

"Okay," I said. "Stick to those topics when you converse with him. Just make it clear to him that at this certain time of the day, you are studying and you need his help to take care of things. But outside of those hours after you study, leave behind anything related to studying. Don't tell him anything about your studies unless he asks or gets curious. Other than that, don't bombard him with all the details." I could tell that Lea could be incessantly talkative, and I could only imagine the headache her husband would have listening to a topic he could not relate to. After a few days, Lea messaged me, saying thanks because it worked! She felt good that she and her husband were back to talking about topics they both loved.

Find other online learners to talk to about your studies with. Don't overwhelm your spouse, family, and friends with this journey that they cannot relate to. Sure, they are your number one support system; these close social relationships are the ones who will help you carry some of the burdens to make studying a bit lighter. They can help you run errands, get groceries, do laundry, clean the house, or take care of kids. Tell them that this is the support you need from them. Yes, you need to be specific because sometimes people cannot guess how to help in the right way. But don't exhaust them with the details about your studies. Only share the details they need when they ask to satisfy their curiosity.

God's Word Is All About Relationships

The emphasis on relationships in Scripture is consistent. From the beginning of the Garden of Eden, God said it is not good for man to be alone. Notice how four out of the ten commandments in the Old Testament were about our relationship with God, and the remaining six were about our relationship with other people. Israel as a nation was subdivided into tribes or families.

There are many stories of close relationships in the Bible. Ruth and Naomi is a story of a relationship between a woman and her mother-in-law. David and Jonathan were two best friends. When Jonathan died, David took care of his crippled son. Elijah and Elisha is a story between a mentor and a protegee, how a calling to be a prophet was passed down to the next person. Job had friends who sat with him when he was suffering and mourning his loss. Job's ten children tragically died and he lost all his properties. Daniel and his friends captivated our attention when they stood up for their faith. They were captives in Babylon, but they refused the order of the king to eat meat. This story shows how a group of friends can make an impact on a kingdom. Even Jesus in the New Testament has three closest disciples, Peter, James, and John. They were privy to his most vulnerable moments, such as when He was praying and sweating with blood in the Garden of Gethsemane. Paul wrote much of the latter part of the New Testament, admonishing all types of relationships, such as servant and master, husband and wife, parents and children, and the church and church leaders. Above all, Jesus regarded the church as His bride, and someday, there will be a grand marriage celebration in heaven. From these examples, we can see that God is, indeed, the inventor of relationships!

Ask for God's Help in Your Relationships

If you are struggling right now with your relationships: spouse, family, friends, professor, other online learners, etc. you can pray and ask the inventor of relationships to intervene for you. First, if these are bad relationships you cannot get out of, such as relationships with your parents or children, ask God to help you learn how to deal with them so that they can be restored to a healthy state. God can redeem and restore broken relationships. On the other hand, if these are relationships you do not have and desire to have, such as good friends or a loving spouse, pray and ask God to lead you to the right people.

I always pray to be in the right relationships. I have prayed for a good, Christian man. God did not only give me that, but He gave me exceedingly, abundantly more than what my heart desired. He gave me great in-laws! I prayed that He would give me friends in my doctoral journey, and He blessed me not only with classmates, but also with professors who are now my colleagues at work! I prayed that He would give me friends in Arizona. Now, I have different circles of friends from work, church, and the barre studio. I can't believe how the Lord has answered my prayers.

This is a broken world. Instead of benefitting and being blessed with close social relationships through immediate families, friends, and communities, many people are traumatized and suffer horrendously through abuse and abandonment. If you have experiences like these, and you still have not healed from them, please do not hesitate to seek professional help such as counseling or therapy. It is not worth risking your future happiness with something that should be left in the past. Process your feelings, engage in self-care, and seek support from those around you.

Meanwhile, many of us may be at that stage where we are continuously building our relationships, hoping they will last forever. Remember my bus ride metaphor. Depending on your life season, always remember that relationships are fluid, and one must keep seeking and building relationships. It is not the end of hope when a relationship ends, such as in a romantic breakup, academic graduation, FO (friendship over), divorce, or a church split. We need to accept that life goes on, and we need to embrace the current season we are in and the relationships we have in it. There will come a day when a season of life ends, i.e., graduation, and people in our close social circle must move on. Thus, we need to keep making friends, building communities, being vulnerable, and being open to new friendships. If possible, cherish and nourish old friendships, even if circumstances have changed. But if a friendship fizzles out and dies a natural death, that is OK. Life goes on.

"Two are better than one, because they have a good reward for their toil. For if they fall, one will lift up his fellow. But woe to him who is alone when he falls and has not another to lift him up! Again, if two lie together, they keep warm, but how can one keep warm alone? And though a man might prevail against one who is alone, two will withstand him—a threefold cord is not quickly broken."
Ecclesiastes 4:9-12 (ESV)

Life Goes On: Keep Building Relationships

I have made many circles of friends at different seasons in my life. I have childhood friends, high school friends, college friends, work friends, academic friends, IVEP friends, and church friends. I have moved a lot in my life. I lost my first best friend in first grade because we moved to another province. To this day, I still haven't found her on social media. When I was a teenager, I was a casualty of a church split, and I lost many friends. I missed their fellowship so much. For years, I isolated myself. I buried myself in books, and spent a lot of time imagining fantasies of brighter days where all would be well and I would get back with my church friends. Many times, I would cry myself to sleep. Eventually, I learned that life goes on.

I learned that life has its seasons, and God will give us people to surround us during a season. Some of them are for that season only, and some might remain for the next one. I learned that I should just enjoy the season and the people I am surrounded with. I give my best shot at relationships, so that when it comes to an end, I live without regrets.

When I moved to Arizona in 2018, I left a community of friends and families in the Philippines. I had best friends at my workplace, at a small group in my church, and a small circle of best friends from my master's cohort that were my constant, solid support. In Arizona, I had nothing. I fell into a season of sadness, albeit depression, when this truth finally sank in. I would take it out on my husband, and it was unfair that I expected him to play all these roles that my friends used to fill up.

Johnny and I got married three weeks after my arrival to the United States thanks to my mother-in-law who did all the wedding planning and arrangements. That helped lessen my anxiety. After the wedding, I needed to wait for a few months to get my work permit, so I had a lot of free time while my husband was at work. But, who do I go with when I want to get my nails done, or when I want to go to a spa and get a massage? Suddenly, I had no girlfriends to go with to explore art galleries or museums. For a time, I did these things all by myself while my husband was at work. Surprisingly, it was actually not that bad. However, I still longed for girlfriends to do these things with. There was a void and empty ache in my heart.

I prayed to God to send me the right people to be friends with. With His grace, I was able to get myself out of that void and started making new friends and building new communities. I started working soon after, and that helped as I made new friends at work. Despite the COVID-19 pandemic that happened, I now have friends at work, friends at church, and met some Filipinos who became my friends, too. The most surprising thing that happened was when Bree, a friend of mine from the Philippines, also moved to Arizona and married someone from Chandler, a nearby town. Now, even our husbands are friends!

Keep Meeting Together!

Close social relationships are not handed to us on a silver platter with a golden spoon. They are built, nourished, and cherished over time. Those enjoying close social relationships have experienced hardships yet have decided to stick together and plow through the hard times. Spending quality time with your children, spouse, family, and friends takes a great amount of effort and also expenses. But this is the only way we can nurture and let these relationships grow. Even the Bible says that we should not give up on meeting together (Hebrews 10:25, NIV). You've probably heard of this verse in church preachings, as speakers will refer to this as the act of going to church. But I believe this also means meeting together in informal or casual settings.

With all the friends I made while studying online, our friendship was sealed when we met in person. When I was taking my master's, the university did not arrange for our meet-ups over dinners or coffee. We had to make an effort to coordinate things on our own. Some of my classmates from other provinces even flew to Manila and checked into hotels just to make it to the meetings. At my doctoral residency, the university did not tell us to create our own group chat and stay in touch. It was our effort and decision to do so. After two years, our group coordinated to meet again in person just to catch up and talk about dissertation writing. This was not planned nor sponsored by the university either.

I hear a lot of online learners complain that they can't make new friends with their online classmates. They blame the university for not coordinating and arranging plans for them to meet. If this is you, I challenge you to take leadership in forming new friendships with your classmates online. You can start a gathering with people that live in nearby areas or cities.

Beware of Social Media Friends

Today, being an influencer on social media is a huge deal. Many have replaced good-quality close social relationships with the number of followers they have. Do not be fooled by this. Followers on social media are fantastic, but they are *not* relationships. They are an audience. They are consumers seeking information and entertainment that they can devour. There are many social media influencers with thousands, even millions of followers. Yet, they have no one to call or talk to when they need a listening ear. Connecting with like-minded people on social media is a good start, but unless you meet in person and spend time together, that is not real friendship.

Let's Wrap It Up!

God values relationships, so ask Him to help you get into the right relationships. Ask God to bless your current relationships and guide you into nourishing and cherishing them. If you are in an abusive, unhealthy relationship, ask Him to give you wisdom on how to set boundaries or get out of it. Life is short, so we must intentionally build healthy, close social relationships. It is crucial to recognize the relationships that genuinely support personal growth and well-being while finding ways to nurture and strengthen them. With God's guidance, you can cultivate fulfilling, close relationships that contribute to the flourishing life God wants you to have.

Part 3

OVERCOME

Focus: Overcoming Internal and External Challenges

"Little children, you are from God and have overcome them, for he who is in you is greater than he who is in the world." 1 John 4:4 (ESV)

Consider getting a degree online as a mountain that you need to conquer and overcome in the next few years of your life. The sooner you accept the reality that there will be hardships and challenges in getting an online degree, the sooner you will be able to place yourself in a position of victory. When you want to climb a mountain, for example, Mt. Rainier in Washington state, you do not go there and start climbing right away. Instead, your successful completion of the trip relies greatly on your preparation. First, you physically prepare your body for months. You may do hikes with increasing levels of difficulty to build your endurance. Next, you also prepare your food, water, clothes, and camping gear. You also research about the trails by watching vloggers who have done it, take mountain climbing courses, and practice survival skills such as how to make a fire, tie a rope, or climb rocks.

Since you are not an expert mountain climber, you will also not go alone. Rather, you will join a group with an expert guide who will give you instructions before you start your climb. You know very well that it is important to listen to the guide's instructions and follow what they say to ensure your safety. Mentally, you will prepare yourself by acknowledging realistic expectations and knowing what and how to think to counter any negative thoughts that may hinder you from successfully reaching the summit. With physical and mental preparations, plus the guidance of an expert mountain climber, and the presence of others who are on the same adventure, you are more certain and assured that you will reach the summit and return safely according to the planned schedule because, *"You're not alone!"*

I often wonder why people who apply into a higher education program online, whether it be a college, masters', or doctoral degree, don't adequately prepare for their academic pursuit. Attrition rates of college students average between 25-30% of dropouts after the first year in college.[12] The statistics for those taking master's and doctoral degrees are even worse.[13] While there are many factors that can be attributed to the dropout rates, being online and feeling isolated is one of the reasons why. However, I feel that there are no serious preparations undertaken by incoming online students regarding the gravity and seriousness of pursuing education online.

Based on personal experiences, I have encountered many students who are surprised at the challenges they encounter in their first course, such as how time-consuming it is, how there are multiple readings to do, how most of their assignments are in writing, and how professors do minimal lectures or teaching. In their minds, they still have the picture of a traditional college classroom where professors are in front of the room giving lectures. And all they have to do is listen, then take the tests to prove their learning. Somehow, they get the shock of their lives when they find out that they have to self-teach, self-explain, and self-discover to learn in an online classroom.

Welcome to online classes. This is the norm. Thus, in this section, you will be given tools to build your endurance and stamina in your academic journey. As mentioned earlier, in mountain climbing, there are

---

12   Spitalniak, Laura. "First-Year Persistence and Retention Hit Decade High." *Higher Ed Dive*, 27 June 2024, highereddive.com/news/first-year-persistence-retention-hit-decade-high/719946/. Accessed 9 July 2025.

13   Young, Sonia N., et al. "Factors Affecting PhD Student Success." *International Journal of Exercise Science*, vol. 12, no. 1, Jan. 2019, pp. 34–45. *PubMed Central*, https://www.ncbi.nlm.nih.gov/pmc/articles/PMC6355122/. Accessed 9 July 2025.

physical and mental preparations. Furthermore, there are materials and tools such as knives, ropes, tents, etc. that will aid the climber all the way to the summit. In the same way, this section will provide you with tools so that you can have stronger stamina and endurance as you climb the summit to a successful completion of your journey in academia.

"No, in all these things we are more than conquerors
through him who loved us." Romans 8:37 (ESV)

Chapter 9

MASTER YOUR MINDSET

> *"Do not be anxious about anything, but in everything by prayer and supplication with thanksgiving let your requests be made known to God. 7 And the peace of God, which surpasses all understanding, will guard your hearts and your minds in Christ Jesus."*
> *Philippians 4:6-7 (ESV)*

"Dr. Mueller, can I submit all my assignments for the week now? There's a hurricane warning and our area is affected. I am afraid we might lose electricity or internet connection. I want to make sure I submit everything before the hurricane passes this way." Jamie was an A+ student; she never had a late submission or failing grade. Of course she can submit early! I love when students work ahead, not behind. Although they are required to participate in the discussion forums over four days in a week, I will allow a student to post everything in one day in case of emergencies like this.

"Dr. Mueller," read another message that popped into my inbox. "A hurricane is on its way in our area. I am sorry, but I cannot submit my assignments this week. We might lose electricity or internet connection. Can I submit them late? Can you please waive the deduction points since this natural disaster is beyond my control?" Karina was already failing in the course. Each week she came up with an excuse for her late submissions. Her pet died. Her brother was sick. She had a lot of work-related meetings. She was traveling. The hurricane only provided a convenient excuse, and she jumped at the opportunity to ask for no penalty for late submissions. The hurricane hadn't even passed yet, and there was still electricity and internet connection. Instead of working ahead, she already succumbed to the worst-case scenario and acted as if it already happened. Victim mode activated.

These student messages were real! Although the wordings above were not verbatim, I would receive similar messages from two types of students experiencing the same thing. One with a strong, healthy mindset is proactive, a leader, does not make excuses, and works ahead. On the other hand, one with a poor mindset plays as a victim even before tragedy strikes, makes excuses, acts helpless, and feels entitled given the circumstances.

The difference between a good student and a poor student is the *mindset*.

Prepare Your Mind

Cultivating a healthy mindset as an online learner can shift one's educational experience from mundane to actively rewarding and enjoyable. First, you must acknowledge the realities in your life and all the possible challenges you will encounter. Assess your situation such as the demands in your full-time job, the attention your children need, the stress of doing household chores, and the quality time you need to take care of your relationships. Maybe you also have disabilities such as ADHD[14] or dyslexia. Or maybe you are dealing with a chronic illness, are the primary caregiver to an aging parent, or are a single parent with no community of support around you. All these are the realities of life, and it is comparable to assessing the terrain of the trails before you go on a big hike. Having an understanding of this terrain is the beginning of your mental preparation paving the way to cultivating a positive mindset.

---

14 Attention Deficit Hyperactivity Disorder (ADHD) is a condition where one is not able to focus or keep still.

Optimistic But Realistic

A positive mindset is optimistic but realistic. I know some people who always say, "Think positively!" or "Be positive!" While their positive attitude is admirable, their actions and the reality of their situation do not align with their optimism. Actually, I sometimes think that they are deceiving themselves with their optimism. Now, that is not a positive statement, but let me cite an example.

I was procrastinating on a difficult assignment. I was positive that, just like before, once I sat down and worked on it, I could finish it in an hour or two. I found a lot of convenient excuses not to work on it. I needed to go to a basketball game with my husband. Our time together was more important, right? I needed to clean the house. An organized environment would clear a cluttered mind, right? Oh, the drawers on my desk needed decluttering, too. That's right, I had some laundry to do as well. Wait, my indoor plants must be repotted. The assignment could be done at a later time.

The day of submission came. I was pretty positive I could still get this done. Three hours before the deadline, my heart started to pound as my anxiety increased. I was perspiring as I realized the assignment was more difficult than I thought. "Lord, I need you! Please help!"

This is not the optimistic mindset that I am talking about. This is plain procrastination–an avoidance and denial of the realistic demands an assignment presents. You may be optimistic that you can juggle everything in your life just like any other people that you know or have seen on social media. You know that there are those who have full-time jobs, kids, disabilities, and a whole lot of other responsibilities, and they've gotten degrees. So there is possibly nothing in this world that can stop you from getting a degree, too.

And that is true! Nothing can truly stop you. But your mind can. Your optimistic outlook is a good start, but you need to match your optimism with the challenges of your reality and mental toughness. You need to acknowledge the rough patches of the terrain so you will keep on keeping on when the going gets tough. Because, you see, the problem I have seen with so many of my students who did not make it past their first year in college was unpreparedness. The going only gets tougher until the very end. And they were not mentally prepared to take on the challenges because, in their minds, it is not something they signed up for. Remember, when the going gets tough, the tough keep going.

So, here's what you should do. Check your optimistic attitude. Then, check in with reality. What is doable for you? For example, you are optimistic that you will be able to catch up with all your late assignments this weekend so you are not worried at all. But then, check in with reality. How fast can you work? How fast can you read? How fast can you write? Can you focus and concentrate without distractions during the amount of time you need to finish your assignments? How is it likely that an emergency can come up and disrupt your flow? For instance, the babysitter does not show up or you lose internet connection. Would you still be able to finish your assignments despite these interruptions? Do not be overly optimistic to the point that you turn a blind eye to the realities of your life that you end up deceiving yourself. When you can give your situation an honest assessment, then your realistic optimism can boost your mental toughness.

"Then you will know the truth, and the truth will set you free."
John 8:32 (NIV)

Grit and Resilience

Cultivate a positive mindset through grit and resilience. Grit and resilience is the ability to persevere and thrive despite setbacks, challenges, and adversities. I like the book of Dr. Angela Duckworth[15] on grit where her research showed that it is not just intelligence that makes students succeed, but it is grit. In one of her studies, students who have higher scores on grit are the ones who survive later rounds in spelling contests. Grit and resilience is having determination, passion, and perseverance towards long-term goals. It is the ability to bounce back and not give up despite failures or challenges.

Online students who succeed in their academic goals are those who grit their teeth when the going gets tough and just keep moving forward. Disappointments and frustrations such as failed tests, failed

---

15   Duckworth, Angela. *Grit: The Power of Passion and Perseverance.* Scribner, 2016.

courses, rejections, delays, financial hardships, and many other external challenges may be experienced during an academic pursuit. But grit is staying focused on the goal, on the bigger picture, and having the ability to keep moving forward.

Getting my Ph.D. made me realize that getting a doctorate degree does not mean being the smartest person. People with doctorate degrees have grit and resilience. There were so many surprising challenges that can hamper the progress of a doctoral learner. For example, in the dissertation process, the committee members can reject your work multiple times and tell you it is not good enough to proceed to the next level. And this can go on for years! Many learners give up before they finish the program because they can no longer bear the corrections and criticisms. There is no question about their intelligence, that's for sure. But the grit and resilience it takes to keep going despite the emotional challenges is the game-changer.

When I started my Ph.D. program, I did not know that I signed up for sleepless nights burning the midnight oil so that I could finish my assignments. I did not know that free weekends were rare, instead spent writing assignments, reading journal articles, and eventually writing dissertation manuscripts. I did not know that I signed up for hot summer weekends, alone in our house in Phoenix, deep diving into data analysis while my husband went up in the mountains with the family where it was cooler to play golf. I thought I would be rewarded by the end of that summer with a done dissertation, enabling me to graduate in October. Instead, I was told that my work was rejected and major revisions must be made. The slight discrepancy in my data distribution calls for Spearman's statistical method, not Pearson's which I used.

My heart sank in exasperation as I recalled all those tables and figures that I had carefully extracted and formatted on the manuscript, along with well-written interpretations. It did not help when I consulted a statistician and was told that my research findings using Pearson's method would remain the same if Spearman's method was used. Thus, the first version was acceptable. "But what would it take for you to graduate?" The statistician asked. "Your committee's approval, correct? So do as they say," was his wise advice.

Ah, the self-pity party I had with tears in my eyes as I sat trying to stay the course in my dissertation journey. I remembered all the pictures on my Facebook feed of my friends and their travels during that summer. It made me more miserable! I sacrificed a whole summer for nothing! I knew that the dissertation was an iterative process, but this one was my biggest rejection. My husband heard my blood-curdling scream as I slammed my fist on my desk.

After I bawled, cried, and threw a silent tantrum, I reminded myself about the person I wanted to become. Yes, it took several days to emotionally recover and get into the right mindset again. I wiped away my tears, straightened my shoulders, and shook all negativities away. Time to get back to work and press forward. Life goes on, and I told myself to keep moving forward by taking one tiny step, one tiny revision at a time until I conquered this mountain under my feet. I literally gritted my teeth and went back to writing. I kept in mind the positive thought that no matter how long, this season, too, will come to pass. And it did!

"Have I not commanded you? Be strong and courageous.
Do not be afraid; do not be discouraged, for the
LORD your God will be with you wherever you go."
Joshua 1:9 (NIV)

My graduation did not happen in October 2023, but on December 20, 2023 of that year, I wrote on my Facebook wall:

Legally and officially.

It is Ph.inisheD. It is Ph.inisheD.

Ph.D. in General Psychology (Emphases in Technology and Learning)

January 16, 2020–December 20, 2023

It took

-3 years

-11 months

-4 days

To pass

-15 courseworks

-2 residencies

-6 dissertation courses

And obtain 8 Levels of Approvals:

1. Research Prospectus Accepted

2. Chapters 1-3 Approved for Defense

3. Proposal Defense Passed

4. IRB Approved for Data Collection

5. AQR Approved Chapters 1-5 for Final Defense

6. Final Defense Passed

7. Form and Format of Manuscript Accepted for Proquest Publication

8. Dean's Read and Signature

With guidance and approval of:

1-dissertation chair

1-content expert

1-methodologist

2-assessment quality reviewers

1-reviewer from the Internal Review Board

2-Form and Format Reviewers of Manuscript for Proquest Publication

1-Dean to sign and make it official!

What a journey it has been to become a

Dr. Remilyn Mueller

"...I know whom I have believed, and I am convinced that He is ABLE..." 2 Timothy 1:12, (NIV).

Self-compassion and Self-integrity

To cultivate a positive mindset, learn how to cultivate self-compassion and self-integrity. There are many people who show compassion to others but are too hard on themselves. There are also many people who have integrity, but they lack self-integrity. Self-compassion is giving yourself some grace. It is forgiving yourself when you make mistakes, when you fail, when you mess up, and when you cannot live up to your standards and meet your own self-expectations. I have encountered many students who struggle with self-compassion. They don't know how to forgive themselves. They get one point deduction for a tiny mistake and they beat themselves up as if they have failed the whole program. Self-compassion as an online learner is giving yourself space to grow, make mistakes, learn from mistakes, and give yourself as many chances as you can when you fail and mess up. Self-compassion is not wallowing in shame for the embarrassing things you have done, such as failing a course or getting reported for a plagiarism issue. Rather, you acknowledge that those things happened, you made grave mistakes, and even though you feel ashamed, you are going to learn lessons from them so you can grow and become a better person.

On the other hand, self-integrity is a problem not so many people realize. It is the grave sin of not showing up for yourself when you said you would. When you agree to meet up with your friend for a coffee, and you show up at the time you said you'd come, that is integrity. People trust you and believe what you say because you have proven repeatedly through time that you are true to your word. What you say, you do.

However, it is sad that while you have integrity in the sight of others, oftentimes, you do not have self-integrity. You do not show up for yourself when you said you would. You said you want to be more healthy so you want to eat healthy food, exercise, and sleep better. However, you don't keep up with this promise to yourself. Your "self" ke3pw waiting and hoping that one day you will do what you promised. But before you know it, years have passed and you still have not kept your word. This is a lack of self-integrity.

As an online learner, you promised yourself that you would not wait until the day of the deadline of the assignment to do it. You told yourself that you will no longer allow your body to experience stress and anxiety just to beat a deadline. You told yourself that you would make your education a priority, manage your time well, and be on top of your assignments so that you can give yourself a break from academic tasks for a day or two each week.

And yet, here you are. Every week goes by the same as it was before. You keep pushing off your assignments to the back burner because other things always come up. You spend time endlessly scrolling on your phone when you should be reading your study materials. You check your social media when you should be writing your assignments. You allow yourself to be distracted by chatting on your messenger while you are writing your assignment. So, the two hours you have each night that were supposed to be devoted to your academic studies have come and gone, and you've barely accomplished any of your goals.

While you may not lack compassion and integrity for others, make sure that you do the same for yourself. A healthy, positive mindset is cultivated when you practice self-compassion and self-integrity.

"May integrity and uprightness protect me,
because my hope, Lord, is in you."
Psalm 25:21 (NIV)

Healthy Coping Mechanisms

A positive mindset is borne from practicing healthy coping mechanisms when challenges arise. When problems, failures, setbacks, challenges, and difficulties arise, choosing healthy coping mechanisms is a game-changer. Modern-day science suggests therapy, counseling, support groups, and meditation among many other things as ways to cope healthily when life throws rocks and a wall hits your face. These are all good, scientific, and proven effective most of the time.

But on a personal note, I find my faith in God, hope in His saving grace, and trust in His Word as effective healthy doses to cope with life's curveballs. When I read His Word and find promises there that He will never leave me nor forsake me, that the battle is His and that the Lord will fight for me, and I only need to be still, I find sweetness and relief in full surrender. I know that I can only do so much, and my rope is too short and its end can come too soon. But at my rope's end, my Savior will meet me and get me to where He wants me to be. I know that He who began a good work in me will bring it to completion (Philippians 1:6, NIV). God's Word tells me not to worry about tomorrow, not to be anxious but instead, by prayer and petition, I can lift up my requests to God (Philippians 4:6, NIV).

"Know that the LORD is God! It is he who made us, and we are his; we are his people, the sheep of his pasture." Psalm 100:3 (NIV)

Find Support Groups.

It is amazing that modern-day, scientific methods for healthy coping mechanisms are deeply rooted in Biblical Christian teachings, but many people don't know or realize it. In Chapter 8, I discussed making friends with other online learners. I want to mention again what the Bible says about not giving up on meeting together (Hebrews 10:25, NIV). Furthermore, Jesus also said that where two or three are gathered together in His name, He will be in the midst of them (Matthew 18:20, NIV). This is the same concept for counseling, therapy, and support groups. You "come together" with another individual or group of counselees so you can talk, share your problems, and gain perspective from a professional.

As an online learner, help yourself cope with academic challenges by finding support groups. Although it is a bit more challenging to find support groups in an online classroom, there is one easy way to start. Find online groups on social media such as Facebook, Instagram, or LinkedIn.

For example, on Facebook, search for online groups for online students from your university. Or, search for online students who are taking the same program as you do. Sometimes, there are also groups for online students based on their race, region, or country. Another way is to form a social media group yourself and invite your classmates from your courses to join. The main idea of this practice is to connect with other online learners who are going through a similar journey as yours.

In the Old Testament, God Himself said that it is not good for a human (Adam) to be alone. In the New Testament, we can read of disciples and the early church who would often gather and strengthen each other in the midst of the unknown as they were being persecuted and executed for their faith. Many times, Jesus would gather His disciples over food! You are not meant to be alone and isolated in your academic journey even though you chose to take the online format. So, find your people. Your tribe is waiting somewhere.

"As iron sharpens iron, so one person sharpens another."
Proverbs 27:17 (NIV)

Self-Reflections

In the Old Testament, many people meditated, such as Abraham, Moses, Job, and King David. Chapter 15 of this book talks more about the practice of self-reflection. Meanwhile, King David had written some of his meditations in Psalms where He expressed anger, disbelief, complaints, and all emotional outbursts to God. However, he often ended his rants with praises and thanksgiving. If our faith fathers who are revered as strong and mighty had to sit back, and meditate, then perhaps, we also need to do the same. When you sit back and reflect on what was, what is, and what should be, you will find answers for the necessary steps needed for you to move forward in the right direction.

It has been more than a year since I finished my Ph.D., and almost two years since I started writing this book project. I feel defeated that so much time has passed, and I have not been productive in achieving my book writing goals. My goal was to finish writing the first draft of this book two months after I finished my Ph.D. I did not anticipate that it would take longer than that. After a year, I have very few pages of writing to boast about. I cannot let my feelings of despair and frustration get the best of me, though. If I did, I would end up avoiding opening this project on my computer.

For self-reflections to be effective, you must write them down. You can pretend that one side of you is the counselor and the other is the counselee in need of help. This practice is similar to neuro-cycling[16]. Here's a snippet of my self-reflection when I felt like a mess for not achieving my writing goals over the months. The process of unraveling what happened made me understand, forgive, and give myself the much-needed grace so I could move forward.

Counselor: So, from December 2023 after you finished your Ph.D. to May of 2024, you have not done much writing for your book. You said walking on your graduation day brought the closure you needed. What about the summer months? Why was there still no progress?

Me: Ah, it started to get so hot that I stayed inside. You know, when I opened my desktop computer, I couldn't write my book because it gave me PTSD[17] from my dissertation writing. I felt like I was going through the whole Ph.D process again. So, I couldn't write. I know that last May, I made progress in writing when I went to coffee shops. But, it's too hot. I was too lazy to get out of the house once I got back from the gym in the morning.

***

Counselor: Well, did you do anything productive at all during these last two months of summer?

Me: Well, I took more adjunct classes and substitution classes. I actually had 12 classes at one point. Imagine, the regular load for faculty is only three classes. But I had 12! That is 4 times more of

---

16   Neurocycling is a mind management technique developed by Dr. Caroline Leaf that helps individuals break down and reframe negative thought patterns and cycles.

17   Post traumatic stress disorder (PTSD) a mental health condition that's caused by an extremely stressful or terrifying event — either being part of it or witnessing it.

my regular teaching load! Then, we would go to Payson on most weekends. We also traveled to New Orleans. There were also days when we would just go out for a drive. And oh, I've read books.

Me *(continues)*: Telling you all of this made me realize that I was productive but in a different way. In other words, my productivity did not contribute to my big goal of writing my book's first draft, so that is why I feel shame and defeat.

Counselor: You know you cannot keep going like this if you want to finish your book before the year ends, right?

Me: Right.

Counselor: OK. This is what you should do. You have done this practice before and it was effective. Write down your daily schedule. Plot the times in your week when you would do some writing.

> *"Search me, God, and know my heart;*
> *test me and know my anxious thoughts.*
> *See if there is any offensive way in me,*
> *and lead me in the way everlasting."*
> Psalm 139:23-24 (NIV)

This is how I self-reflect. I look back on the past to process what happened. Indeed, you cannot undo the past, but understanding what happened will make you forgive yourself and give yourself more grace so you can keep moving forward in the right direction. Now that you are reading this book, you probably think that that was the last writer's block I had experienced. That is incorrect. After a month of writing spree, I got busy with other stuff again when the fall semester started and the holiday season brought events and activities. It took some time before I realized that I should never say that I don't have time to write my book. I should say that I have time to do other stuff and writing my book was not one of them. I had to keep going back to the neurocycling process of beckoning myself to sit on my chair, and opening the document to finish writing this book.

By now, you know that this self-reflection and how I processed my predicament helped me finish this book. When you fail a course, get a bad grade, or generally feel defeated, sit down and WRITE what happened. Don't just think about it. Let it out. Name your enemy and call it out so that it will no longer taunt and mock you. God bless you as you reflect and call on His favor and grace so you can keep moving forward with a mind captivated by Christ.

Failures Can Happen

Failures can happen. But failing does not have to be the end of your story. A positive mindset regards such occurrences as a redirection, maybe a wake-up call, but it is not the final outcome. There were many moments in my life when I felt like a failure in my academic journey. I never failed a course, yet I failed finishing a master's program once. That redirected me to an online program that allowed me to be free on weekends and yet work on my master's degree at the same time.

Then, another failure happened again when I failed to finish the first doctoral program I enrolled in when I was in the Philippines. Years later, God gave me a second chance here in the US and I finished it. Looking back, I know that I did not finish my first master's program offered on a traditional campus so that I could experience what it was like to be an online student. That experience as an online student helped me relate to my students when I got an online teaching job. And what about the Ph.D. program I did not finish in the Philippines? Well, those courses I took gave me leverage to teach communication courses at the undergraduate level. Looking back, these two perceived failures serve their purpose to lead me to where I am supposed to be today. Failures can happen, but don't let them be the end of your story.

> *"My flesh and my heart may fail, but God is the strength of my heart and my portion forever." Psalm 73:26 (NIV)*

Attitude of Gratitude

Lastly, always have an attitude of gratitude. Gratitude is a habitual practice to focus and appreciate the positive aspects of life despite all the negativities around us. As an online learner, it is so easy to divert our attention to negative things in our online classes.

*The professor's feedback is vague.

*There are too many readings, assignments, and all sorts of deadlines.

*My classmates are boring and discussion forums are dead.

*Why did I get points deducted on my citations?

*I wish my professor would break down the information and provide more instructional videos, TikTok style.

These things may be true, and if you focus on them, they will only grow in your head and will turn you into an unhappy, disgruntled person. Try to find things to be grateful for. When I was studying, I would also complain a lot. I even voiced out my complaints to people around me like my friends, my husband, and family. It was nice when they validated my feelings and gave encouraging words. However, I would not wonder if they, at some point, got tired of hearing me rant about my dissertation. During my Ph.D., I read Ann Voskamp's book, *One Thousand Gifts,* where she listed one thousand gifts that she is thankful for, and explained the anatomy of gratitude. I tried to emulate her example and listed down things I was grateful for. It was hard at first, but before I knew it, my countless list grew. When I finished my Ph.D., I got to the point where I was truly thankful for my dissertation committee and the whole iterative process, because they sharpened me to do beyond what I thought I would never be able to do such as explain the statistical analyses. Hello, numbers!

Five Things I Was Thankful for during My Ph.D.

1. Support system. My husband and family supported me in this endeavor.

2. The opportunity to study. Many people want to but they don't have this opportunity.

3. Tuition benefit. As an employee, I got 75% of my tuition covered.

4. Resources. There are many resources available to do my research.

5. Time. My full-time job is online, and this gave me more time to study. The pandemic allowed me to focus and not be distracted by travels and social events.

Gratitude impacts your daily choices and your daily choices impact the outcome of your future. When you reach a point where complaining seems to be natural and appropriate in your situation, try to jolt yourself and direct your mind to take the gratitude route. I would say prayers of thanks, and rebuke the seed of discontent that the enemy tried to grow in my heart and head. I would pray something like,

"Lord, thank you that you who began a good work in me will bring it to completion. Thank you that you said in Your Word that you will fight for me. You told me to take courage and be strong. I am so tired, Lord. But in your Word, you invite me to come to you because your yoke is easy and your burden is light. I am laying my burdens to you, Lord. Thank you that you already promised victory through your Son, Jesus Christ. Amen![18]"

When I pray God's Word out loud, my outlook changes, and my heart and head feel lighter. Suddenly, there's renewed strength and motivation to keep going until I see light at the end of the dark tunnel I'm in.

Let's Wrap It Up!

Online learners usually set goals for themselves, often with high expectations. Optimism, if unrealistic, can lead to disappointment and a feeling of failure. Realistic optimism means acknowledging the challenges and truths of life without denying them. Develop grit and resilience, the determination to persist and bounce back from setbacks. Rest if you need to but never give up. Self-compassion and self-integrity are essential for self-preservation. Be kind and gentle with yourself and show the same understanding as you would with others. Show up for yourself in your pursuit of goals. That is self-integrity. Control what's within your reach

---

18   If you want to look up the full verses in this prayer, please go to Philippians 1:6, Exodus 14:14, Joshua 1:9, Matthew 11:28:30, and 1 Corinthians 15:57.)

and surrender what you cannot change. Failures can happen but let it not be the end of your story. Lastly, have an attitude of gratitude and pray God's Word over your life. Keep pushing forward. Never give up on your dreams, and keep trying until you reach your goals.

"Trust in the Lord with all your heart,
and lean not on your own understanding.
In all your ways submit to him,
and he will make your paths straight."
Proverbs 3:5-6 (NIV)

Chapter 10

SPEAK LIFE, BUILD BRIDGES

"Do not let any unwholesome talk come out of your mouths, but only what is helpful for building others up according to their needs, that it may benefit those who listen." Ephesians 4:29 (NIV)

If there is one thing I realized when I got married, it is how bad I can be at communication, which is a shame considering that I have a communication degree. It is the way I phrase my questions. For example, I would say, "Did you throw away the leftovers?" My husband expressed how that sounds as if I am already accusing him. So, I asked. "How do you want me to say this better?" He said, "Well, you could say, 'Where did you put the leftovers?'"

Same message but communicated differently.

Communication is a vital component of any successful relationship. In an academic setting, effective communication enhances relationships with peers and superiors. It paves the way to a flourishing life. On the other hand, bad communication can lead to conflict. Conflict should be avoided at all costs because it can escalate quickly if not handled well.

One way to handle conflict is to stress the importance of remaining respectful, apologizing when necessary, and seeking a constructive path forward.

Sometimes, online learners also have to deal with combative classmates. This usually happens on a collaborative, group assignment. Triggers can lead to conflict, and you must be aware of these cues. Do you want to work ahead and submit before the deadline because procrastination triggers your anxiety? You need to communicate that. There may be some people in your group who procrastinate and will not do their part until the deadline. In all cases, humility is the key element for academic success.

Layers of Communication

There are many layers of communication. As an online learner, we will focus on four areas of communication that you often use as a student: reading, writing, listening, and speaking. The majority, if not all of your output, will be in writing. A few requirements might ask you to speak, usually by creating an audio, such as a podcast episode for an assignment, or a video. You will also spend a lot of time reading materials such as journal articles, books, instructions, professor's posts, classmates' posts, etc. At times, you will also listen to video or audio materials such as instructor videos, inspirational talks, educational podcasts, etc. Writing and speaking skills are productive skills, while reading and listening are receptive skills. When you write or speak, you produce information that you want to communicate to others. When you read or listen, you receive information from what others have produced.

Reading Skills

Reading is an active and engaging receptive skill. In an online learning platform, there are multiple resources built into the class. When you see numerous resources, do not panic and think that you have to go through each one. There are strategies you can apply so that you can make the most out of it. First, look at all the tasks that you have to accomplish for the week. What do they require? For example, if the discussion question asks you to explain what financial management is, you don't have to read all of the 20 materials about financial management. Skim and scan one material at a time, and once you spot a page or section that will help you answer the assignment, go ahead and read that section in detail so that you can do your assignment correctly.

Imagine yourself in a buffet restaurant. When you enter the buffet area where all the food is spread out, you scan and survey the tables. You know that your stomach has a limited capacity so you want to make sure that you make the best out of the buffet experience by choosing only the food that you like best. You pick a small portion of each chosen dish and go back to your table to taste them. When you like something, you can go back for seconds, or you go back to try other food. Pretty soon you are full and you cannot take in any more food, but you are satisfied because you chose the food that best served you at the moment. Treat the list of course materials as a buffet table. First, you skim and scan the reading materials and pick the ones that you think will help you finish the graded tasks for the week. Then, when you have more time, you can go back to the other materials that are on the list. Even though you were not able to read everything thoroughly, you are satisfied knowing that you have finished all the graded tasks on time.

A note of caution though. There are things that you should read thoroughly. Never apply the principle of skimming and scanning when you read announcements, assignment instructions, or course policies. Remember, there are many tiny details there that are so important that can put your grades at risk. Some tiny details that students often miss are word count requirements, number of paragraphs required in an essay, etc. Professors get frustrated when they get messages asking questions that were already discussed in one of their announcements or course policies. When students ask questions that are already discussed in detail, it is a sign that they have not done their due diligence in reading.

Do you know that in the Bible, Paul admonished Timothy to devote himself to public reading of the Scripture? Why is a snippet about reading so important that it had to be inserted in the Scripture? The following two words in the verse gave the clues: exhortation and teaching. When you read, you learn from others. The more you know, the more you will grow as a person. When you grow, the more you can exhort and teach others with wisdom and discernment.

"Until I come, devote yourself to the public reading of Scripture, to preaching and to teaching." 1 Timothy 4:13 (NIV)

Writing Skills

Writing is a productive skill that involves a rigorous process. In Chapter 20, I discussed a section about writing as a transferable skill. You cannot pour from an empty cup. So, if you are struggling with what to write when given a certain topic, for example in a discussion forum, that means your cup is empty. Go and fill it up by reading about the topic first. Do not reach out for a quick Google search or ChatGPT. Since you are writing an academic paper, look for peer-reviewed academic resources such as journal articles. Or look for the materials provided in your course. This takes a lot of discipline and determination on your part because reading academic resources is no reading for pleasure. It can be quite painful. Writing is like childbirth. Ah, it can be so painful and frustrating, but it brings joy and a sense of accomplishment once you are done with it. No wonder a lot of students call their thesis or dissertation their *baby*.

As an online learner, never say that you are not good at writing. When you say that, you are already putting yourself in the position of defeat. Say that you are a determined learner and you are going to write better and better every single time. Pay attention to the words you use, the way you structure your sentences, the way you weave one sentence to the next, and the way you connect one paragraph to the next. Academic writing follows a standard formatting structure. An example of a formatting style is APA 7. Check with your university or professor regarding the formatting style required for your paper. Most of the time, this is already stated in the course policies or announcements. After you are done writing, before you submit it, pretend that you are now the reader. Read aloud what you wrote. Be your own critic. Does your writing sound clear, concise, and sensible? Revise as often as needed. Revisions are OK and necessary because even the best writers make revisions countless times before they get accepted for publication.

Your writing lives on long before you are gone. Think of the Bible, classic literature, and archived documents. The authors of these have long been gone and yet their writing still impacts our lives today. As a learner, thank God for the opportunity to hone your writing skills when you do your academic tasks and assignments. Pray and ask God to help you. Who knows, maybe one of His plans for you is to write something valuable that would impact future generations beyond your lifetime.

"...my tongue is the pen of a skillful writer." Psalm 45:1b (NIV)

Speaking Skills

Speaking is another productive skill. One section in Chapter 20 also talked about speaking as one of the transferable skills. However, do you know that public speaking is one of the top ten fears of people? Public speaking is the most common requirement in traditional campus classes. This can include presentations in front of the class, debates, group discussions, or class recitations. However, for online learners, other forms of speaking requirements may include live online presentations, creating reels or videos, creating a podcast, or responding to discussion questions in a short video clip. Most confident speakers start by writing first what they want to say and practicing it a couple times before the real presentation. One way to improve your speaking skills is by taking a video of yourself during these practice rounds and, just like in writing, you play it back and watch yourself as your own critic.

Don't be too hard on yourself, though. You may find yourself fumbling or stuttering in fear and nervousness. But don't worry. Nervousness and fear of speaking is normal. Do the thing you fear. Even the best speakers get nervous. But do you know that nervousness can be a good sign? It means that you are taking this task seriously.

When I was in college, one of my professors told me that once I get up on stage and start talking, it is normal to be nervous in the first five minutes. However, after five minutes, that nervousness should disappear. If you are nervous all throughout your speech, then that is not a good sign. So what do I do so that my nervousness will disappear within the first five minutes? My professor said, "Make sure you prepare well."

When you prepare for a speech, it does not mean writing a full script and reading it aloud word for word. Reading a script is not a good practice for public speaking. It is not engaging. An engaging public speaker should not read nor memorize a full script. What you should memorize is the outline of your main points. When you know the main points by heart, you will be able to sail through your entire speech with or without the script or the PowerPoint slides to guide you. Here's a list of things you should memorize:

1. Your introduction or opening spiel.

2. All your main points.

3. Information that you will emphasize in each main point.

4. How you will transition from one main point to another (connectors).

5. How to close or end your speech.

Remember, whether you are speaking from a stage or platform like they do in traditional classrooms, or presenting online through technology, you are imparting something to your audience. Make sure you are imparting something worthy of their time. It should be something that builds them up, or something that they could think about as their takeaway.

"My heart is stirred by a noble theme as I recite my verses for the king..."
Psalm 45:1a (NIV)

Listening Skills

Listening is a receptive skill, and you might think it is a mindless thing to do. However, you will use this skill whenever you listen to videos, podcasts, or lectures. Cultivating your listening skills now will be an asset in your personal relationships and even in your professional life. Many components of listening require tact and talent. For example, can you think of a person who knows the right words to say, or remembers what you said a couple of weeks ago? Or do you know someone who gave you a perfect gift because they remembered something you said that hinted at what you liked many moons ago? Or, do you know someone who knows that you meant the opposite when you said you were fine just because they could read your body language such as facial expressions and body movements? People who can empathize, understand, and respond properly to human needs have good listening skills, and they pay good attention to what is being communicated in a situation.

Listening is a complex receptive skill that involves many layers. It is different from merely hearing what the person said. It is interpreting words and making meaning by combining this with other factors such as context, culture, body language, and relationships. As an online learner, sometimes this is the communication skill that has less opportunities for development and practice. In an online learning environment, listening is often only used when course material is in video or audio form. And in this case, there are many times when students do not listen with their full attention because they are doing something else, like driving, while the video or audio is playing. Nonetheless, you can sharpen your listening skills in your everyday conversation with others.

Technology for Reading, Listening, Speaking, and Writing

In Chapter 14, I discussed technology as one of university resources that you can utilize. In recent years, developments in AI (Artificial Intelligence) technologies that aid reading, listening, speaking, and writing are astounding. One feature in your smartphone can allow you to record a speaker or an audio, and turn it into text so you can read it later. If you are taking your dog for a walk, running on a treadmill, or on a two-hour drive somewhere, you can use voice notes to speak and this feature would turn your speech into texts that you could edit and revise later for your discussion questions, participation, or assignment. This feature also includes a summary if you want to summarize a long speech into short, main points.

Another feature on your smartphone can also help you with your reading. You can choose any reading material from your course and this bot will read it for you as you listen. There are also AIs that help you summarize long journal articles; this is very helpful when you are writing a research paper. Then, there are also AIs that can help you write. Think of them as a brainstorming partner. You can ask an AI for main points aligned to the topic you are writing about and it will give you ideas. You should not copy and paste the AI output as it is. But you should check other sources such as journal articles that will support the ideas the AI provided. Then, structure your writing around what AI suggested that academic journals also supported.

You either love or hate technology. But they are here to stay and they will only keep improving. As an online learner who is committed to lifelong learning, learn how to utilize some or at least one AI that can help develop your communication skills. Artificial intelligence will never replace humans. But if you don't know how to use it, then other humans who know how to use AI will replace you.

How to Communicate Effectively with Your Professor

While most students go through their college years without experiencing a conflict with their professor, some do, and this is not uncommon. Miscommunication can happen in an online environment and can escalate ugly emotions real quick. If your exchange of messages is starting to escalate into a conflict, here are a few things to keep in mind.

Assess the situation. First, you need to stay calm and assess the situation. Ask yourself if this situation is worth fighting or arguing with. Choose your battles because not all battles are worth your precious time. Are you fighting for 2 points taken off from the rubric despite the detailed explanation on why they were taken off? Maybe you just have to let it go. However, if those two points will give you a passing mark in the final grade, then yes, it is a battle worth fighting for. You see what I mean? Ask yourself why you want to battle it out.

Remain calm and professional. Remember that just because you are a student does not mean that you are not an adult or a professional. Act like one. Remain objective. Do not make unnecessary insertions of the personal dramas happening in your life such as getting sick, going through a tough time such as a messy divorce, moving across the states, losing a job, etc. Of course, all these affect your temper and your patience to remain calm and professional. And who knows, your human professor is probably going through the same personal dramas and their fuse is also short. So, focus on the problem and resolve for a solution to fix it. (Forgive me for calling it *drama*.)

Identify and state clearly what the problem is. Many times, a conflict starts when students expect their professor to solve their personal problems or lavish them with extraordinary favor when they fail to meet requirements. One of my recent experiences was about a student who sent me a long message and said one of her aunts who was very close to her was in hospice. She described her relationship with her aunt from childhood to the present (I skimmed and scanned through that whole thing), and seeing nothing that concerns an action on my part, I made a quick response saying, "Thanks for the information!" She got so angry at me and reported me to my manager saying that I was rude and not compassionate. In hindsight, I realized I could have said, "I am sorry you are going through this. Is there anything I can help you with?" But that morning, I was also in a rush with grading and wanted to finish answering all student messages because I needed to leave for a meeting on campus. Seeing that she was not asking me to do anything to help her, I just replied with a quick acknowledgement.

In this example, what do you think her and my problem was? In hindsight, I think she could not finish an assignment and wanted an extension for its upcoming deadline. But nowhere in her message did she mention this. When you message your professors, state what your problem is and the help you need from them. If it is a problem they cannot solve for you, then it is useless to inform them about it. The problem on my part was not reading between the lines that she was asking for an extension of a deadline.

Clearly state the "action" you expect from your professor. When students write long messages sharing personal situations, most professors skim through the long message looking for that *line* that particularly calls for an action on their part. In the incident I mentioned above, had the student asked for an extension of the deadline for the assignment, or a university resource that offers counseling for grieving students, then I would have known how to help her in a productive way. When messaging your professor, make it short, simple, and clearly state the action you want your professor to do.

Follow this pattern. State the problem, then state what you want the professor to do to help you. Problem + Action = Effective Communication. This writing pattern is so simple and very effective in communicating your needs and expectations. For example, if you cannot understand the assignment, don't just message your professor saying, "I don't understand the assignment." First, this statement is too vague and the professor does not know which part you do not understand (assuming that you read all the instructions). The professor would likely ask, "Which part do you not understand?" When students answer, "All of it," it is more likely, number one, the student has poor comprehension skills and is not fit for that higher education program, or number two, the student did not really seek to understand the instructions, look for resources provided, and watch the video explaining the assignment.

As a college instructor for many years, I can guarantee that it is only *part* of an instruction that students do not understand and need clarity on. Otherwise, either one of the two reasons I stated above is true. So when you write to your professor, start by saying the problem, "I do not understand the second part of the assignment. What does this particular line mean, "Use this sheet to answer number 4? Can you please explain which sheet you are referring to?" If this is the way a student frames the question, the professor can immediately respond with a specific answer that will help the student. No time will be wasted sending messages back and forth. It helps reduce the probability of misunderstanding and frustration from both sides.

Here's a simple pattern you should follow when messaging them.

1. Say your greetings: (Dear Professor,)

2. State the problem. (I was not able to submit my assignment last night.)

3. State the action you want your professor to do. (Please allow me to submit it late.)

4. Sign off with a thank you.

That's it! No need to explain your predicament or situation with a long dramatic message.

Note of caution: Now, some professors are the opposite. Some would ask for an explanation; they want you to convince them that you should be allowed to submit an assignment late. If this is the case, go ahead and use your persuasive skills to convince your professor to do what you want them to do for you. But it is safe to start with a simple message and not the other way around.

How to Deal With Combative Classmates

In Chapter 20, conflict management is one of the transferable skills discussed. Just like on traditional face-to-face campuses, conflict between students can also happen in online classes. For example, some students would argue in discussion threads. One would copy another's post, tweaking a few words here and there to change it a little bit. Sometimes, a student can be too critical and disrespectful of another's posts, and it sparks conflict and creates a hostile online environment.

At all times, avoid being the instigator of conflict. If you need to argue or present an opposing perspective, do so respectfully without sounding critical or hostile toward another person. Comment on the concept the person presented, and avoid attacking the person. If you are not sure how to do this, maybe it is better to avoid responding at all. Always remember to be kind and gentle when entering into dialogues in class discussions.

When I was in my master's class, we had to do a group project. Now, this was really hard because all of us were working and had our own schedules. It was difficult to agree on a time to meet online and discuss our plans. There were five of us, and except for one, everybody tried to make it work. Everybody, except for this one person, did their part. I was the one assigned to put everything together, and with our deadline fast approaching, I was in panic mode when this one classmate was unresponsive. Now, part of the instruction for this group project was to work it out with each other and not bother the professor to intervene in problems like this, because we were all adults and were expected to solve individual differences and conflicts.

So, I consulted the other group members and we agreed to give him the ultimatum. I was tasked to message the person. I said I know life is busy and he may not have the time to work on our project. However, the deadline was fast approaching, and we wanted to submit it on time to avoid a penalty for late submission or possibly failing and retaking the course. I said that if he did not respond in 24 hours, I would go ahead and do his part, and then submit the project. However, I would also write in the report that he did not attend the meetings nor contribute any to our project. That is when he started being combative saying I'm an a**** for giving him an ultimatum when the deadline is still a few weeks away. I explained that he could not wait until the deadline of the submission before he did his part, because I needed time to put it together. With his combative attitude and my patience running out, we had an ugly encounter.

Looking back, I know that giving him the ultimatum was right. What I should have avoided was the back-and-forth messages. I should not have made those rebuttals to his accusations because I placed myself on the defensive side. He should have been the one defending himself for not collaborating during the planning phase. After informing him about his ultimatum, I should have just kept my peace. What I also did right was I kept a record of all our meetings, and all the group messages, and our individual messages to each other when he started attacking me. I filed this together and included it in our report as evidence of him not participating. In the end, he did not submit anything, so the rest of our group divided his work among ourselves to finish the project.

When you encounter a combative classmate, you would be wise if you knew when to stop your rebuttals and keep your peace. You don't have to stoop low. One option is to report this classmate to your professor, or if there is a student service that handles student complaints, let them do the job. The best thing about online classes is you most likely would not meet this classmate in person and would probably never encounter them again. And depending on the gravity or nature of their bullying towards you, you can choose to keep your peace to focus your attention and direct your energy to higher purposes that will reach your goals.

Protect Your Personal Information

With so many scammers, fraud, and online stalkers that exist, online learning platforms are not spared. Be sure that you do not give away your personal information, such as in the class introductions, for the rest of your classmates to know. Information such as home addresses, email addresses, and phone numbers must not be shared because universities use these as your identifying information when you make or take a call from the school. In short, you do not want your classmates to know this information because they can call the school pretending to be you by using this identifying information.

If you don't want your classmates to find your personal social media accounts, change your social media name to something more discreet and not with your official name in the class. If you want to stay connected with your online classmates or professor, but you do not want them to pry on your personal life and see your non-academic related activities such as beach vacations, create a LinkedIn profile and direct them to contact you from there.

Let's Wrap It Up!

Communication aspects in reading, writing, speaking, and listening are all intertwined. Reading and listening are receptive skills while writing and speaking are productive skills. You need to develop and sharpen all these skills to succeed as an online learner. The recent developments in artificial intelligence technologies can help you in your reading, writing, speaking, and listening activities. There are features on smartphones that can help you convert your speech into text. This feature is wonderful because you can be talking about an assignment while you are walking the dog, and lateryou can convert this recorded speech into texts. With some editing and revisions, you can have a finished assignment in no time.

One aspect of communication as an online learner is communicating with your professor. Remember to communicate respectfully and clearly. Avoid getting into the habit of making excuses by narrating the personal dramas in your life just to get an extension of a deadline. The simple formula for structuring your message for your professor is Problem + Action = Effective Communication. This means that you state the problem you want the professor to solve. If your problem is something the professor cannot solve, such as being sick, then you do not have to message your professor. But if you have missed an assignment because you were sick, then state the problem as "I missed submitting the assignment." The action you want your professor to do is allow you to submit it late. So say, "Can you allow me to submit it late?" If your professor asks you for further explanation, then that is when you divulge the details. Always remain calm and professional and avoid conflict. Avoid combative classmates, too, and refuse heated exchange of messages. Lastly, when communicating within your online classrooms, protect your personal information. Do not give your home address, phone number, email address, etc. If you want to connect with people in your online classes, create an email, social media account, or LinkedIn profile where you can connect with them.

Chapter 11

MONEY TALKS— ARE YOU LISTENING?

"If any of you lacks wisdom, you should ask God, who gives generously to all without finding fault, and it will be given to you," James 1:5 (NIV)

I was appalled when I came to the United States and learned about the gravity of student loans and their impact on the financial health of graduates. As an outsider looking in, I thought the government was awesome for lending money to people who wanted to study. At first, I was impressed to know that students not only get money to pay for their tuition, but they can also get a check to pay for their living allowance while studying. This means that they don't have to work while studying, right? I was envious. Then, I also learned that as long as they keep studying, they can defer payments. So, after a bachelor's degree, they jump right to their master's degree and so on. Wow! I was amazed!

But not for long. When I learned that most of them owe $100,000 to $250,000, my admiration turned to shock! Everything looked so great to me until I learned that many of them do not earn enough to pay this off easily. Some take as much as ten to twenty years! Paying back these loans was a struggle and gave them a rough start to life. They got their first paycheck after getting a degree, and here it was slashed with deductions to pay off their student loans. Not fun!

This Is What We Can Afford

In the Philippines, tuition fees are paid in cash either by the parents/guardians or by scholarships. Before I started college, my parents sat me down and told me that they could only afford to send me to a local college, not to one of the big universities in Manila. So, while my high school classmates were scrambling to apply to prestigious universities in Manila, I was set to wing it at the local college. Attending a university in Manila not only meant paying for tuition fees five to ten times as much, but it also meant paying for transportation, dormitory, books, clothes, and other expenses. Our meager family income was way less than that total expense. My parents told me that our goal was for me to *just finish college.*

"And once you have your degree," my mom said, "Find a job. Then once you are earning your own money, you can fund and pursue whatever dreams you have." I fancied becoming a writer, so my first choice was a journalism degree. At the local college where I was set to go, they didn't have a journalism program. The question that remained was, "Which program should I take if they don't offer journalism?" My very wise parents told me sternly, "Choose a degree that will get you a good job." At that time, I was terrified of math courses. So the program that didn't have a lot of math courses and would guarantee me a job after graduation was an Elementary Education degree.

My dad would skimp and save so I could pay the full tuition every semester. I enrolled the full load which was 7-8 classes a week (Monday-Saturday) because that would save money in fees for miscellaneous, library, athletics, etc. I did not live in a dormitory, but I would commute back and forth for 1.5-2 hours total through public transportation every day. I would bring lunch, or have some crackers in my bag. My spending allowance was just enough for transportation and a simple lunch, so in order to save, I would skip lunch on some days of the week and wait until I got home to eat. That strategy worked, and the savings I got from my lunch money on those days were for unexpected expenses that might incur such as course projects.

My mom stayed home to take care of the family, but she was also busy doing a lot of side hustles to earn money. I remember that I was on the last hurrah of my student teaching days, and I was worried about the extra expenses my final teaching demonstrations would incur. "Mom," I said hesitantly. "I need to prepare food for the other teachers and my professors who are coming to observe me." She beamed excitedly and replied, "Don't worry. Tell me what I can do. I have money saved for this event."

I gritted and ground, and in three and a half years, with summer classes included, I was able to finish a four-year degree. I did not think that this hardship would impact me later in life. But college taught me to live within my means and make do with what I can afford, not what I like or prefer. My likes and preferences can only come if I can pay it in full. To this day, I practice this, and I am so thankful the Lord gave me a spouse who shares the same financial views. We agreed to only spend what we have and not get into debt. For example, when we travel, we save up for it and pay the credit card bill in full.

I worked my way up from teaching at the elementary level to teaching in college. Several years later, I was able to finish my master's degree at an online program from a prestigious university in the Philippines. This time, I was earning well and I paid for my own education in cash. When I was working on my master's degree, I met some classmates who were from other countries. And when I asked why they chose a university from a third-world country, their response was because the tuition was cheaper and more affordable compared to getting the same degree in their country. From what I last heard from them, their master's degrees from the Philippines were recognized in their countries, and they were able to pursue their dream jobs with that degree. Perhaps like me, they also live by the principle of sticking to what they can afford.

Several years later, I became even more ambitious and wanted to pursue my Ph.D. from a first-world country. My first choice was New Zealand. I passed the rigorous application process at a university and I was able to secure an advisor for my proposed research. Now, the next part of the process was what stalled me: the funding plan. I applied for a prestigious scholarship that would cover most of my expenses and got shortlisted. Sadly, I did not get the cut to the top 25 applicants. The university told me my other option was to take student loans. I did not like that, so my dreams of getting a Ph.D. in New Zealand went down the drain.

A year later after that rejection, I met Johnny, so I forgot my Ph.D. dream for a while. However, when I applied for a teaching job in Arizona, that Ph.D. I thought I had forgotten, leaped on my face the first day I went to the university for the job interview. I walked down the hallway and a sign said, *Welcome to the Doctoral Zone*. I got the full-time online teaching job, and along with it came the tuition benefit for full-time employees. Seven months later, I started my Ph.D. with that scholarship. After four years, I graduated. Again, no student loans. No debt. Because God provided faithfully.

I have faith that if you ask God to give you wisdom, you can also get a degree without getting into so much debt. It is God's Word that says, *Owe no man anything,* and *The borrower is a slave to the lender.* It is Biblical not to get into debt. I am sure God wants His children to be debt-free.

"Owe no one anything…" Romans 13:8a (ESV)
"…the borrower is slave to the lender." Proverbs 22:7 (ESV)

Scholarships

One good thing in the US and other first-world countries is the multiple scholarships that are available. In the Philippines, there were very few scholarships available, and since my dad had a stable job, I was disqualified. They were given to those whose parents had no stable jobs or financial means to pay for tuition. And usually, those scholarships are so meager that they will not cover all college expenses. So, I did not bother to get into the long line of thousands of other applicants at the governor's office to apply for college scholarships.

But here in the US, you can apply for scholarships online. There are scholarships for veterans, for nurses, for teachers, etc. There are employers who offer college scholarships to their employees as part of their benefits. Then, some foundations also offer scholarships. Try to look for scholarships that will help cover, either fully or partially, your tuition and other university fees. If your employer does not offer scholarships, then look for a job that will! Usually, jobs at universities offer either partial or full scholarships.

> *"No one from the east or the west*
> *or from the desert can exalt themselves.*
> *It is God who judges:*
> *He brings one down, he exalts another."*
> *Psalm 75:6-7 (NIV)*

Students Loans

If you have student loans, here is some unsolicited advice. Do not treat your student loans as an income. There are many students who enroll just to get the monthly stipend as if it were their source of income. Yes, I have had students who would tell me not to fail them or they would lose their monthly stipend. To persuade me even more, they would say they didn't know where they would get the money to buy food and pay their rent if they failed my course. To get a monthly stipend is a wrong motivation to study.

What I will tell you next is something unethical for me to tell my students as their professor. But as my book reader, I will tell you that if getting a monthly stipend is your motivation for enrolling in a higher education program, then you are better off just looking for a real job. If this is your big 'why,' then there is a possibility that you will end up not finishing your degree. You will end up poorer than when you first enrolled, and with debts. Some people have $25,000 to $30,000 of debt without a degree because they failed their initial courses and they cannot move forward. As my reader, I honestly tell you now that there are some people not cut out for academic studies. This means they will prosper somewhere else because their gifts and calling are different. I can usually spot who these people are after two weeks of classes. I wish that as a professor it was ethical to tell them that they are not going to make it.

If possible, get a real job to pay for your living expenses, and do not cash that monthly stipend. Remember, that stipend is not an income. It is a loan, and you will pay it with interest right after you graduate. Take the minimal amount of loan that you can. Also, discuss with your financial adviser from the university about the ramifications of student loans. If you withdraw from a class that has already started, or if you failed a class, there might be an out-of-pocket expense for you. Be ready for out-of-pocket expenses. Some students feel crushed and cannot continue when they cannot afford to pay for something that student loans cannot cover.

After the first course, here are some signs students are not going to make it:

1. They got a D or C in their first course. (This is the first course. It is the easiest. If their grade is this low, it's time to evaluate if academic pursuit is right for them.)

2. If they got a D or C in their first course, there's a big chance they will fail their second course. If they fail their second course, it is time to step on the brake.

3. They still cannot figure out how to navigate the online course portal despite watching all the video tutorials. Their posts go in the wrong places. They cannot view feedback from an assignment because they don't know where to look. They just can't figure it out on their own. And when they do, they forget the steps next time they try again.

4. They have no computer or reliable laptop. The one they have keeps crashing on them.

5. They have no internet connection. So, they do schoolwork on their phone.

6. They don't know how to manage Microsoft Word documents. Their professor always says that they submitted a blank template. But they really did their work. Now, where did it go? They can't find it.

7. They just can't figure out the style format i.e. APA and how to do in-text citations.

8. They hate writing. And they just don't understand what the professor means by the need to organize ideas, mind grammar, and writing mechanics. They write the way they speak, so why is

the professor nitpicking on these things?

9. They can't understand instructions or how to use templates. Ah, they hate templates, and they don't know why the professor keeps saying that the document they submitted is distorted.

10. They need their professor to call them and tell them what to do. They just can't comprehend written instructions or feedback, or even video lectures.

Please Note: I feel that writing these tell-tale signs is harsh and blunt. If these describe you, please know that I am not trying to put you down. My intention is to keep you from accumulating debts in your student loans. God's plan for us is not limited to academic achievements. I am sure He has better plans for you and He will show you if you ask Him.

Explore Abroad

Explore opportunities abroad. If you are feeling a bit adventurous, maybe an online program from a university abroad is something more affordable for you. There are many immigrants here in the US who got their degrees abroad and they are paid the same. Those who got their degrees in the US are struggling to pay student loans while these immigrants have none. If this is hard for you to believe, look at teachers, nurses, and doctors in your community or inner cities. Listen to people in technical support services. A lot of Americans think they will not find a job in the US if their degree is not from an American university. The truth is, there are many top universities even from third-world countries that offer quality education. If immigrants can come to the US and find jobs, what is the likelihood that a US citizen cannot find a job in their own country if they studied abroad?

To drive home a point, when I was teaching in the Philippines, I had some foreign students in my class mixed in with their Filipino classmates. There was a time when the economy in Greece was in bad shape, and we had an influx of Greek students because they could not afford their education in Greece. And then there were also Filipino Americans whose parents sent them to the Philippines to study engineering, nursing, business, etc. because the parents did not want them to incur student debts in the United States.

Today, online programs are rampant, and these opportunities can provide a way for you to get an affordable degree from abroad without leaving the United States. Hint: Look at universities from countries such as the Philippines, Thailand, Vietnam, Indonesia, and Brunei to get you started in your search.

Financial Literacy in a Nutshell

Finances are needed to meet basic needs such as food, housing, healthcare, and education. As an online learner, you may need to work fewer hours to have more time to study; thus, impacting your finances. Or, as mentioned before, you may need to take out student loans to fund your studies. Whatever your case may be, studying impacts your finances. I am not a financial literacy coach or guru like Dave Ramsey, JL Collins, or Toby Mathis, to name a few, but I like reading books about financial literacy. And with all the advice out there, here are some financial goals that you can start working on right now as a student: Tithe, save, invest. I am just helping you get started, so focus on these three.

Tithes and offerings. If you love the Lord and want to obey Him, you know that giving back to Him is an act of worship. God is a faithful provider and giving back to Him through tithes and offerings tests our faith. Sometimes, it is hard to let go of a couple bucks in the offering plate, and it is easier to spend them on entertainment or food. In the end, your willingness to give speaks more about your heart than your pocket. Include in your budget what you are going to give to the Lord. Don't just give him some change from your pocket when the offering plate is passed your way.

Save money. Savings should come first before spending. Look at savings as if it is a monthly bill. You save first, then you spend the leftovers. It should not be the other way around. Now, there are different purposes for saving money. But just to get you started, save money for no reason at all. Some people think there should be a reason for saving money such as for travels or home repairs. They save to spend. What about just getting into the habit of saving, and not touching it until it grows to a certain amount? For example, you can save six months' worth of your income.

So, if you earn $10,000 a month, your saving goal should be $60,000.

Invest. After you save six months' worth of your income, invest. There are many forms of investment. You can choose which works for you. You can add more to your 401K, start a Roth IRA, or a regular brokerage account and invest in the stock market. Just to get started with investing, buy index funds or ETFs (Exchange-Traded Funds). They track top companies in the US and you don't have to spend time studying the financial health of an individual company. As you acquire the discipline of investing, you will learn more about the stock market and you can explore other options in investing.

Set a budget. There you have the first three things you can do to get started with your financial management: tithe, save, invest. Include these in your budget. Remember, it is not the amount. It is the discipline in these financial habits that you should acquire. If you think you don't have enough resources or money for these, list down all your expenses and cut off the unnecessary ones. Look at your subscriptions, takeouts, and entertainment expenses. You will be surprised at how much you spend on unnecessary things. Even a daily coffee worth $5 is a total of $1,825, and a $20 takeout every day is $7,300 in a year! I am not saying that you should not get coffee or takeout. What I am saying is to be aware of these small expenses. They are worth a lot when accumulated in a year.

Tithe. Save. Invest. This is a good start! Educate yourself more about financial and wealth management after you graduate. Then, you can create a plan to pay off your student loans, earn more, and retire with a comfortable and generous life.

Flourishing and Finances

VanderWeele[19] suggested that financial and material stability sustains flourishing. In the previous chapters, you have read about happiness and life satisfaction; mental and physical health; character, virtues, and values; meaning and purpose; and close social relationships. All these are domains of flourishing. Nonetheless, it makes sense that finances are

---

19   VanderWeele, Tyler J. "On the Promotion of Human Flourishing." *Proceedings of the National Academy of Sciences*, vol. 114, no. 31, 1 Aug. 2017, pp. 8148–56. *Proceedings of the National Academy of Sciences*, doi:10.1073/pnas.1702996114. Accessed 9 July 2025.

needed to sustain these. Finances are means by which we can obtain or access resources needed to support the other things that matter to our well-being. Finances are a driving factor when pursuing personal and professional goals.

Financial and material stability creates a feeling of freedom, a sense of security, and a form of control. It enables us to give back to communities, make a difference, and choose better options. Financial resources are one of the means to make dreams come true and have a better future. Many people need help to become better stewards of their finances so they can have freedom and more options when making decisions.

Unfortunately, financial management is not commonly taught in schools or practiced at home at a young age. Many Americans appear well-to-do, but behind the wealthy facade are looming mortgages, credit card bills, loans, and other debts. One time, I remarked to my husband that people should stop saying, "I bought a car. I bought a house. I bought this and that," if they acquired these material things through credit cards or loans. It is technically not bought. It is loaned. And when something is loaned, it is not owned. No matter what season of life you are in, remember: it is not too late to take control of your finances.

Wealth Does Not Equate Flourishing

So, while flourishing studies have recognized that financial and material wealth is necessary to flourish, they have also concluded that it is not a means to an end. This is very interesting to me. I came across a study about flourishing conducted in five countries–the USA, China, Sri Lanka, Cambodia, and Mexico[20]. This study has proven that financial wealth does not guarantee higher levels of flourishing or well-being.

Participants from the USA scored the highest in financial and material stability. However, they scored the lowest in mental and physical health; character and virtue; meaning and purpose; and close social relationships. The only country that scored lower than the USA in terms of happiness and life satisfaction is Sri Lanka. People from China, Cambodia, and

20 Weziak-Bialowolska, Dorota, Eileen McNeely, and Tyler J. VanderWeele. "Human Flourishing in Cross-Cultural Settings: Evidence from the United States, China, Sri Lanka, Cambodia, and Mexico." *Frontiers in Psychology*, vol. 10, 2019, article 1269, https://www.frontiersin.org/articles/10.3389/fpsyg.2019.01269/full. Accessed 9 July 2025.

Mexico had lower scores in financial and material stability. But they scored higher in all other domains. In short, Chinese, Cambodians, and Mexicans may be poorer than Americans, but they are happier, more satisfied, have better mental and physical health; stronger in character, virtues, and values; have clearer meaning and purpose; and have better close social relationships.

The Love of Money

One of the most popular yet misunderstood verses from the Bible is, "The love of money is the root of all evil…" (1 Timothy 6:10). The extreme misinterpretation of some faith groups is that having money is wrong, so that they would take a vow of poverty. Notwithstanding, it is the love for money that becomes the root of all evil. In other words, the heart and mindset towards money must be put in check so that motives and intentions remain pure. Money can become a master, an idol that some people worship more than they worship God. That is why Matthew 6:24 warned that we should not serve two masters—God and money.

Finances can be the test of any relationships and leadership. Hence, always keep the perspectives and attitudes toward money in constant check. Dangerous shifts can happen anytime! The Bible challenges believers to give back to the Lord and see if He will not open the windows of heaven and pour out a blessing (Malachi 3:10). This is the only verse in the Bible where God challenges us to test Him. And the test is to give generously!

The intention behind giving can be tricky. God always looks into the heart of the giver, and He can see the intentions and motivations of the heart. If you are giving with the intention of getting a blessing back, then that is wrong. God is not pleased. Sometimes, the desire and the quest to be financially and materially stable can be consuming. Hence, remember Ecclesiastes 5:10, admonishing us that money can never satisfy, and wealth is just vanity. Have the right mindset and attitude towards your finances. God bless you as you become a good steward of His resources.

Let's Wrap It Up!

Spend below your means. Stick to what you can afford, and if you are taking student loans, take only the minimum. Look for scholarships. And if education in the USA is too expensive for you, explore options abroad. Be financially literate. Tithe. Save. Invest. The goal is for you to form good financial disciplines and habits. Remember, money will not make you happy. Research has shown that other areas of well-being, such as mental and physical health, meaning and purpose, and close social relationships are more important for a person to flourish. Finances are just a means to sustain them. Nonetheless, the Scriptures also pointed out that we should live and give generously. Giving back is the only verse in the Bible where God dared humans to test Him!

Chapter 12

TIME—YOUR MOST VALUABLE CURRENCY

> *"But seek first the kingdom of God and His righteousness, and all these things will be added to you." Matthew 6:33 (ESV)*

"I don't have enough time!" For many years, it was my convenient excuse for not accomplishing what I said I wanted to do. I wanted to teach Sunday school to young children, but I didn't have enough time. I wanted to be more consistent with my prayers and devotions, but I didn't have enough time. I wanted to visit my grandfather living on his farm eight hours away, but I didn't have enough time. Years passed and the hard lesson I learned was I will never have enough time for things I don't give time for. When my grandfather passed away, I felt awful that I lost my chance forever. Years taught me to manage my time better by creating a schedule and prioritizing what I value most. In Chapter 17, I discuss more about priorities.

Today, I still hear the same phrase from many of my students.

Time management for academic success is a crucial skill. It begins with identifying and prioritizing tasks in the order of their importance. Doing this maintains a clear focus on what truly matters. Treating studying as a part-time job can be a game-changer. Plan your schedules and dedicate time for studying. Be proactive rather than reactive. Vacations, natural disasters, or family schedules are not excuses for neglecting academic responsibilities. Be accountable and responsible. Discipline yourself and exercise effective time management.

What Helped Me

I am a proponent of writing down goals for the year, for the month, for the week, and for the day. I am also into the habit of plotting down my weekly schedule by the hour. My schedule keeps changing as I go through different seasons in life. In fact, my schedule changes depending on the literal seasons of the year: spring, summer, fall, and winter. For example, during fall and winter, we have basketball games. In the summer, we go to Payson on most weekends. My schedule looked different when I was doing my Ph.D., compared to now that I am done. I have an Excel sheet where I have my daily routines plotted down, and what I should be doing on certain days. For example, I grade submissions of major assignments on Thursdays for my doctoral learners because the deadline for their assignments is on Wednesday nights. My regular meetings are scheduled on Tuesdays and Wednesdays. Aside from my job, I also plotted down my schedule for when I would do passion projects such as writing this book. I reserve my Saturdays and Sundays for recreational purposes.

Plan Your Schedule

It is helpful to have a visual reminder of things you have on schedule. You need to get it out of your head and put it on paper. Let's assume that getting a degree is your major priority right now. But then, you also have a full-time job, children, and spouse to take care of. On a spreadsheet (MS Excel), on the first column, plot the hours of the day from the hour you wake up (e.g. 5:00 AM), to the hour you go to bed (e.g. 9:00 PM). Then on the horizontal column, plot Monday-Sunday. Fill in each block of hours with what you should do. For example, if your full-time job is from 8:00 AM to 4:00 PM, then highlight that as one block. Outside of those hours, find the time when you can study. You should also include other things you need to do such as cooking, picking up groceries, having time with your spouse, etc. Remember, if it is something you value, put it in your schedule.

Studying Is Like a Part-Time Job

As mentioned before, treat your studies as if it is a part-time job. You will need approximately 15 to 20 hours a week, remember? That is four hours a day, with a weekend off from schoolwork. That means plotting four hours of your day into your weekday calendar. It can be two hours early in the morning and two hours at noon. Or, all four hours at night. When I was writing my dissertation, there was a time when I broke down my schedule of four hours throughout the day. But it was not effective because I found it hard to get back into writing.

What worked for me was plotting it from 7:00 PM to 12:00 AM. These were my "holy hours" where my mind would just work wonders and my writing flowed in great momentum. Most of the time, the flow was so great that I would keep on writing until 2:00 AM or 3:00 AM. Of course, this schedule is not for a lifetime, it was only for that season when I was deep into dissertation writing. After achieving my educational goals, I worked on getting back to sleeping by 9:00 PM and getting 8 hours of sleep.

Be Proactive, Not Reactive

Life happens! If you are going to spend four to five years getting a degree, expect that life happens and things outside your academic goals can change and impact your scholastic momentum. Now, there are life changes that you can and cannot control. There are things that can wait after you get your degree, and there are urgent things that you must address now as you are getting a degree.

Things you can control. There are some things you can hold back and control. For example, you can avoid changing jobs or accepting job promotions. Changing jobs or getting promoted while you are studying are exciting and can be very tempting, especially if there is a higher pay and better benefits. However, changing jobs or getting a job promotion might stall your academic progress. If your current job is paying the bills and is enough for you to get by, stay at it and focus on your studies first.

Believe me, job opportunities come and go, and more will be available for you after you graduate.

When you change jobs, you need to work harder to make a good impression on your employer and new colleagues. You need to adjust to the new work culture and prove your worth to the new company that hired you. This can take an emotional, intellectual, and physical toll on you. The same thing happens when you accept a new role or job promotion. You have to spend time learning new things, doing the job right, and get stressed at the pressure of performing above expectations. Before you know it, your academic goals will go down a few knots in your list of priorities. So, before you allow changes to happen in your life, first, ask if this is something that can wait. For others, it may not be about job changes. It can be about getting married, having kids, moving across states or countries, or going on a vacation. Before you make a decision, consider how these would impact your studies.

Things you cannot control. There are also things that you cannot control. Sometimes, members of your family will come up with something that can disrupt your schedule such as a parent-teacher conference, or a spouse's work event that you need to attend. You need to give allowance in your schedule for these life events that you do not want to miss with your loved ones. Remember, they should be your priority, too. You have to be wise in gauging if this is something that you truly do not want to miss. Then, you need to adjust your schedule for studying and move it around your calendar.

Recently, a lot of students have encountered issues with internet connectivity when natural disasters happen. I suggest that if there is a bad weather forecast, work on your school assignments ahead of time. If there is a hurricane landing on the weekend when a major paper is due, then work ahead, not behind. Submit before the hurricane comes because, more than likely, you will lose electricity and internet connection. Anticipate the worst and prepare for it.

I remember that while I was studying for my master's degree, there was a typhoon coming. Unlike traditional classes where face-to-face meetings are canceled when a typhoon hits the country, online classes are never canceled and life goes on as usual. Knowing that the typhoon was about to hit us in two days, I scrambled to get my week's worth of assignments done and submitted all of them four days early. True enough, we lost electricity and internet connection. Two things paid off by working hard to submit four days early. One, my grades were not affected. Two, I did not have to worry about submitting my assignments when we lost electricity and internet connection.

Never, ever use the things beyond your control to shirk from your responsibilities and use them as excuses. If you do, the truthful statement is, "Studying was not my priority at that moment. Sorry for slacking in this area." And as a professor, that is fine with me as long as you know that it was a matter of your priorities that made you slack in your studies. I appreciate it when students own their lapses and take full responsibility to get caught up or take the consequences wholeheartedly such as deduction in late submissions. What I do not appreciate is when students are combative, expecting special treatment or favors for their late submissions just because they have an excuse that is beyond their control. There is no such thing as a valid or not valid excuse. An excuse is an excuse, and students use it as a ticket to avoid consequences for their decisions and choices.

Time for Coffee!

There was one video about time management on the internet that left an impact on me. A professor had tennis balls, golf balls, marbles, sand, a cup of coffee, and a small jar on his table. He asked his students if all these could fit in a jar. A lot of students were pessimistic, while some were not sure they would all fit in. The professor proceeded to put the tennis balls inside the jar. Then, he placed the golf balls, followed by the marbles. He shook the jar and each ball found their place between each other in the jar. Next, he asked if the cup of sand would still fit in. This time, the students were more positive. He shook the jar as he scooped sand and they made their way around the tennis balls, golf balls, and marbles. The jar was full! However, he asked if a cup of coffee would still fit in. The students cheered, and the professor slowly dumped the cup of coffee inside the jar. Everything looked snug and nothing was spilled.

The professor then explained that the tennis balls were the biggest priorities in life. As an online learner, what are your top three biggest priorities? These could be job, family, and studies. You should put these first in your schedule. Then, the golf balls are the secondary priorities. These could be your exercise routines, social events, church ministry, etc. Put these in your schedule. But if they clash with your schedule for your top three priorities, you know that you have to find another time for them. For example, if a girls' dinner coincides with the night when your assignment is due, then you need to either finish your assignment early or give up on that dinner with your girlfriends. The marbles represent the little things, but are also important such as doing the laundry, cleaning the house, making dinner, etc. The sand represents all the other things that come up in life such as chatting with friends, answering calls or text messages, etc. These are also important, but you could squeeze them around your tennis balls, golf balls, and marbles. Lastly, the cup of coffee. When you have everything in place because of good time management, you will always find time to have a cup of coffee with a friend!

I think this little story aligns with God's Word where Jesus says that we should seek God's kingdom first and then the rest will be added to us (Matthew 6:33, NIV). I have mentioned this verse a couple of times in the previous chapters. If we prioritize the agenda that truly matters to God, He will make sure He enables us to find strength and time to accomplish them. And He will even allow us to breathe and have coffee with a friend!

Let's Wrap It Up!

Effective time management is key to academic success, starting with identifying and prioritizing tasks. By organizing these tasks in order of importance, you can stay focused on what truly matters—treating studying like a part-time job, dedicating 15-20 hours per week. Schedule specific study sessions, while also allowing flexibility as life circumstances change. It's important to be proactive in managing time, avoiding excuses such as personal events or unforeseen circumstances, and maintaining accountability for academic responsibilities.

Creating a structured schedule is vital for balancing academics with other life responsibilities. Plotting daily goals and scheduling study time can help prioritize academic work. However, life events, both controllable and uncontrollable, can disrupt schedules. Manage what you can control, like staying with your current job or adjusting your schedule ahead of life disruption. Recognizing the difference between what is within your control and what isn't allows for better decision-making without using external circumstances as excuses for neglecting responsibilities.

Chapter 13

UNLOCK THE POWER OF UNIVERSITY RESOURCES

> *"But my God shall supply all your need according to his riches in glory by Christ Jesus." Philippians 4:19 (KJV)*

Back in the day, missing a day of class meant missing out on information. The professor could have discussed something included in the test. If you were absent, you could fail. Students would write notes furiously. Usually, there was only one textbook used as the source of information. Library meant physical books, but there was a limit to what you could take out and borrow. But today, things have totally changed!

Explore the University Student Services

When you enrolled in your program for the first time, the person who assisted you to get started probably discussed all the university student services available. This information overload can be overwhelming, so regularly check with your enrollment advisor or counselor about the university resources available to you. Sometimes, there are new resources that they may have forgotten to communicate to you. Or, they could have emailed it to you and you did not pay attention to reading it.

Tutorials. Some universities offer tutorials. Some offer it for free but with limited sessions, while others ask for a fee. Some of these tutorials are for difficult classes such as in mathematics, science, or writing. Regardless, it is important to know what is available so that when you encounter difficulties, you know that it is not the end of the rope and you can look for resources that will help you pass a course and keep moving forward.

Webinars. Most of the time, universities will offer webinars, or seminars on an online platform, for their online students. Sometimes, these webinars are offered by the library with topics ranging from how to use the online library, how to cite sources, how to write an academic essay, how to utilize artificial intelligence in writing, etc. Sometimes webinars are offered by colleges to talk about course or program-specific issues. Open your eyes for opportunities like this and make sure that you grab them when you can. These webinars will not only give you additional knowledge and wisdom, but you will also feel motivated and inspired as you engage with other attendees. Throughout my academic journey, I have met other webinar attendees who are now part of my contacts on LinkedIn or social media. Some of them graduated the same time I did, and it was a sweet reunion. Years after graduation, I still meet up with them whenever they are in my city or I am in theirs.

Counseling. Mental health is important. Most universities have resources for students who may need counseling. Ask if there are free counseling sessions that you can avail. Even if you don't need it, if it is free, try it. Sometimes, you don't know you need or would benefit from it until you try it out. One of my friends tried a free counseling session. She was surprised at the insights she gained. "I know you guys have been telling me what to do for a long time but somehow it didn't stick with me. But when the counselor mentioned it, it was a lightbulb moment!"

Mental health support. Many universities value mental health and they provide support for students. Ask what is available for you. Take care of your mental health no matter how busy your academic life gets. Your mental health is part of the engine that drives your life. A failure in an engine can bring your life to a crash.

Mentoring. Some universities have opportunities for one-on-one mentoring between a student and a faculty. First, you should know what area of your life you want to grow and be mentored in. Is it in research? Is it in business, finance, engineering, mathematics, teaching, dancing, sports, or fitness? Before you look for a mentor, take a hard look at your life and decide which area you want to be mentored in. Choose one area of focus for now and look for a mentor. Having a mentor means being vulnerable and open to correction and training. It requires trust in the process. Some faculty look for students to mentor. As a student, you can do the same. If you feel that you are learning a lot from one of your teachers, ask him or her if they can mentor you. I had different mentors at different seasons in my life. The most recent one was when I was writing my dissertation. I had to go out of my way and talk to some professors to mentor me.

One way of approaching a faculty member is by attending one of their webinars, asking them questions, and establishing relationships with them. You will discover if there is a good dynamic between you. Respect, appreciation, and trust should be established for the mentoring relationship to work well. Do not choose someone to be your mentor just because they make you feel good. A mentor should be able to speak hard truths in your life, yet at the same time, train and motivate you to stay the course. Do not settle for getting good feedback and praise alone. Make sure the one you choose is willing to correct you and tell you what you are doing wrong. There should be a good balance of both. To succeed in your chosen profession, be open to getting a mentor.

Online Libraries

Make sure that you optimize the use of online libraries. Online libraries in your university usually have access to databases of journal articles, and other research materials; thus, they are available for student use. Part of your school fees include a library fee. Universities pay huge amounts to have access to these databases. So, use it. You paid for it. Next time you pay for tuition, look at the receipt and the breakdown of the fees. How much are you charged for library use? Thus, utilize what you paid for.

Sometimes, Google Scholar is so much easier to use than the university library. Call your tech support and ask how you can link your Google Scholar to your library account. When you find an article in your Google Scholar and it asks for a fee, look if it has a copy from your library. Sometimes, you can request the library to order it for you at no additional cost.

Special Accommodations

If you have special needs, let your enrollment counselor know. Most universities have accommodations for those with disabilities. Many students with disabilities suffer with additional stress due to upcoming deadlines. Special accommodations can extend deadlines for your submission without incurring a late penalty. When you ask if a university has disability accommodations, you need to apply for them. The office will require you to submit documentation such as a doctor's note, lab results, etc. before they approve it. In the US, there are also accommodations for pregnant women. Check with your university about the different categories of accommodations they may have. You might be qualified for one of them. I always tell my students, especially pregnant women, that even if they feel like they do not need accommodations, they should still apply for them and put themselves in the system. That way in case of emergencies, they can use it as a backup plan already in place. Again, work ahead not behind.

Writing Centers

Since an online program is heavy in writing, most universities have established writing centers that support students to get better at writing academic papers. From writing a regular academic paper, to capstones, theses, or dissertations, most universities have available resources. Inquire at your university. If they do not have this, there are many social media groups for learners where resources for writing are posted. Join these social media groups. Post a question to ask if anyone could help you with your particular writing needs. Many members jump in and help generously. My favorite writing center is Purdue OWL. This is free and can be easily found with a quick Google search.

Online Clubs or Organizations

One of the things that online learners miss out on compared to college students who attend face-to-face traditional campuses is the opportunity to join clubs or organizations. Clubs and organizations that cater to your interests give opportunities to network with like-minded people. Now, while it is true that most universities usually do not design and provide clubs and organizations for their online learners, there are opportunities out there that provide the same benefit for you. There are many foundations or charitable organizations that are relevant to your degree or field of interest.

Social media groups. The first thing you can consider is the social media groups for learners. There are plenty out there, and most of the time memberships are free. Joining these social media groups was an incredible experience. These are the avenues where I met most of the amazing people I know who eventually became my lifelong friends. As mentioned before, social media groups can be categorized based on your university, profession, program, or niche of interest. You can look it up by location such as "Educators in Phoenix," or you can be more specific such as "Kindergarten teachers in Phoenix." This is a good way to meet people and make friends. You can collaborate with others to do things together in person such as volunteering for a charitable organization in the area, or maybe just simply meeting in person in a nice restaurant. A word of caution: Just like anywhere else, you need to watch out for yourself and your safety when meeting with strangers.

Local organizations/ foundations. Look for a local organization or foundation relevant to your field of interest or future profession and volunteer there. This is a great way to gain experience in a field or industry you want to work in in the future. You can also network with other like-minded individuals. You can volunteer at a local school, a local hospital, a food bank, a local shelter, etc. One of the women in my church's small group is an empty nester. She loves babies, so she volunteers at hospitals as a baby cuddler a couple hours a week. There are many opportunities to join an organization that would hone your skills and experience. In Chapter 18, I have a section discussing volunteer work and how it can help you gain work experience you can add to your resume.

Where God Leads, He Provides

Always remember this: where God leads, He provides. If He led you this far in your academic journey, you need to trust Him and have faith that He will provide everything you need. Ask Him for wisdom to pave the way for you to find those resources that He prepared for you. You need to look around, ask, knock, and search. Open your eyes to see the provisions around you.

Let's Wrap It Up!

Online learners have access to a wealth of resources within the university ecosystem to enhance their educational journey. Key services include tutorials, webinars, counseling, and mentoring, each designed to support academic success and personal development. Tutorials could address challenging subjects like math or writing, while webinars offer valuable insights on topics such as library usage, academic writing, and more. Counseling services, often free or subsidized, provide critical mental health support while mentoring fosters growth in specific areas of interest. Writing centers are essential for honing academic writing skills, a vital component of online education. Additionally, online libraries linked to tools like Google Scholar grant cost-effective access to a vast array of academic resources.

You can also engage with social and academic communities to enrich your online learning experience. Joining clubs, organizations, or social media groups offers opportunities to connect with like-minded peers, network professionally, and build lifelong relationships. For those with special needs, universities often provide accommodations such as extended deadlines to ensure equitable learning conditions. Volunteering with local organizations or participating in online communities can provide valuable hands-on experience and foster a sense of belonging. These resources collectively empower online learners to succeed academically while cultivating meaningful connections and personal growth.

"Ask and it will be given to you; seek and you will find; knock and the door will be opened to you. For everyone who asks receives; the one who seeks finds; and to the one who knocks, the door will be opened."
Matthew 7:7-8 (NIV)

Chapter 14

TECH-SAVVY, PURPOSE-DRIVEN

> *"Let the wise listen and add to their learning, and let the discerning get guidance." Proverbs 1:5 (NIV)*

I squinted my eyes in disbelief! I could not believe what I just downloaded from a student's submission. It was a *picture* of her handwritten assignment on a pad of paper! She copied the headings and tables from the assignment template and answered them on a physical paper! Then, she took a picture of it and submitted it for her assignment. I was both furious and amused. I will not describe what happened with this case and will leave that to your imagination.

But can you guess what her problem was? *Technology*!

Technology plays a fundamental role in modern education. In Chapter 10, I discussed technologies in education and how they enhance reading, listening, writing, and speaking skills. Having access to a reliable computer and internet connection is a requirement, not an option. Added to the mix is the growing impact of artificial intelligence (AI) in education. Let me repeat this: artificial intelligence will not replace professionals, but professionals who don't know how to use AI will be replaced by those who do. Overall, technology is a learnable and adaptable skill. As an online learner, you should reframe your mindset to grow in technology readiness and acceptance. Resisting technology is counterproductive because it is here to stay. Avoiding it, like that student who used a pad of paper, will not help you grow as a person. Embracing technology enhances your educational experience and opens doors to new possibilities for you. By the way, to save some of your wild imaginations, that student did not make it to the end of the course and eventually dropped out of school. Technology for her was too much, and it was a total hindrance for her to move forward.

Computer and the Internet Connection

Online education relies heavily on both a good computer and a reliable internet connection. These two are requirements to ensure good communication between students and professors. Online students also do collaborative projects, post in discussion forums, or give and receive feedback on their work. Video conferencing and real-time communication with clear audio and video quality rely on a good computer and a reliable internet connection. Seamless interaction is vital for building rapport and support in an academic community that enhances the learning experience.

Cybersecurity and glitch-free. Updated technology prevents security threats and technical glitches that might otherwise disrupt your learning process. A good computer with updated versions of software protects you against malware and other cybersecurity threats, securing your personal and academic data. A stable internet connection minimizes the risk of data loss or corruption during online interactions and file transfers.

Seamless access to your online resources. Most importantly, you need a good computer and a reliable internet connection to access your online resources and educational tools. These resources include your learning management system or platform, digital libraries, academic databases, and various educational applications. A good computer ensures compatibility with these tools, while a reliable internet connection guarantees that access is consistent and uninterrupted. Together, these elements contribute to a smoother, more effective learning experience, ultimately supporting academic success.

Computer. Please note that I said "computer." This can be a desktop computer or a laptop. Not a tablet, ipad, or cellphone. A good computer and a reliable internet connection is important for you to succeed as an online student. A good computer allows you to run softwares and applications smoothly. Some of your online courses will require you to use specific programs for writing, research, or multimedia projects. A good computer can handle these demands without lagging or crashing while you are in the middle of your work! Additionally, a good computer is efficient when you multitask, such as when you switch between tasks and applications. A good computer enhances your productivity and reduces possible frustrations when dealing with outdated computers. Investing in a personal computer is a *must* for online learners. If possible, avoid sharing or using public computers, as this practice can lead to security and privacy issues.

Internet connection. Gone were the days when a lack of internet connection was used as an excuse. A reliable internet connection helps you access your course materials and participate in live virtual classes without fear of getting disconnected while on it. Online learning platforms often involve streaming video lectures, participating in live discussions, and downloading or uploading large files. A stable and fast internet connection ensures that these activities occur without interruptions, allowing you to fully engage in your coursework. Frequent disconnections or slow speeds can lead to missed information, unnecessary stress and anxiety, and the inability to perform your best as an online learner.

Note: If you do not have a good computer and internet connection, then online learning is not for you. Do not use this as an excuse. Do not expect to get special treatment from your professors. Do not ask for an alternative way to submit your assignment.

Artificial Intelligence

Artificial intelligence (AI) is transforming various sectors, and education is no exception. As AI technologies continue to advance, integrating them into the educational systems is inevitable because of the significant benefits it offers. It is here to stay. So, understanding and utilizing it properly to keep academic integrity intact is important for you as an online learner. AI in the context of education enhances personalized learning experiences, improves administrative efficiency, and prepares students for a future where AI will be prevalent. I use AI in a lot of ways, and I know when students just copied and pasted AI-generated texts. The reason why I know is because I know how to use AI. I am fairly acquainted with what it can generate and how it forms sentences.

Personalized learning experiences. Traditional education methods often use a one-size-fits-all approach, which may not address the varying learning styles and paces of students. On the other hand, AI-powered platforms can analyze student performance data to identify strengths and weaknesses. With these, customized resources and exercises that cater to your unique needs can be offered. For example, adaptive learning systems use AI to adjust the difficulty of questions based on a student's progress, ensuring that they are neither overwhelmed nor under-challenged. This personalized approach can significantly improve learning outcomes by addressing the specific needs of each student.

Improves efficiency. AI can streamline logistics, freeing up some of your valuable time. AI can handle tasks such as scheduling, organizing study materials, and tracking deadlines. AI-powered tools can assist with giving feedback on your work before you submit it to your professor for grading. You can use AI to ask questions when studying for a test, or ask it to give you ideas when you are stuck in writing a paper. When you make mistakes on a test, ask AI to explain it to you. This helps you save time waiting for your professor to respond.

ChatGPT was still pretty rugged when I used it to practice for my dissertation's final defense. But it helped me prepare and practice for my presentation. I asked the possible questions my committee could ask me and it gave me answers. It also helped me with a lot of concepts in statistics when I was doing data analysis. I was scared that my dissertation committee would ask me to defend why I chose a certain methodology or design and discarded the others. So, I asked ChatGPT about the differences between these concepts and when they are appropriate and not appropriate to use. It was my tutor! Practicing my final dissertation defense with AI gave me extra confidence knowing that I got all the possible questions covered.

Future with AI. The future job market needs professionals who have skills in using AI. AI is continuously evolving, getting better, and more effective as more industries and sectors adapt it. Getting yourself familiar with AI tools and concepts will place you at a competitive advantage in the job market. In Chapter 18, I discuss transferable skills, and AI skills are definitely one of them! Having skills in the use of AI will help you stay ahead and prepare for careers where it plays a critical role. Yes, I understand that many people, which may include you, have misgivings and doubts about the use of AI. But let me emphasize that it is here to stay. It can never replace humans. But humans who know how to use AI will replace others who don't. It's up to you which one you want to be.

Technology Readiness and Acceptance

As an online learner, you must have an open mind and willingness to adapt to technology. Technology readiness and acceptance means being prepared to use and adopt new technology. There are some factors that impact your level of technology readiness and acceptance. Some of these are your current skills and knowledge, the available infrastructure, and your attitude and mindset.

When you embrace opportunities to learn new technologies, your learning experiences will be enhanced. New technologies such as virtual reality (VR) or interactive simulations, bring innovative tools and resources that are immersive and engaging, helping you understand faster and better the complex concepts in science, medicine, engineering, business, etc. Furthermore, it equips you to advance in your career. The job market is looking for job applicants who are familiar with a wide range of technologies. If you are proficient with tools such as data analysis software, collaborative platforms, and emerging tech trends, you are going to attract good employers who offer great competitive compensation packages. Or better yet, you can be an entrepreneur within the field of your education, optimizing the use of technologies. By embracing new technologies, you are not only staying relevant, but you are also developing critical skills that are highly valued. Technology can sometimes be uncomfortable, but it is the discomfort that gives you opportunities to grow.

The Fear of the Lord

You live at such a time as this. Even though technology can be misused in ways that displease the Lord, I believe that God wants us to model how it can be used for His glory. If you find yourself resisting technology, check your attitude. Sometimes the reason why it is hard for you to learn technology is because you have already set in your mind that you don't like it. If you find it challenging to learn technology, exercise your faith and trust that the Lord will help you through this. The book of Proverbs in the Bible teaches about getting wisdom and knowledge. On the contrary, the *fools and unwise*, as the writer describes them, despise wisdom and instruction. If you fear the Lord, you know that keeping abreast with technology will help further the work of God's Kingdom for the current and future generations.

"The fear of the LORD is the beginning of knowledge, but fools despise wisdom and instruction." Proverbs 1:7 (NIV)

Let's Wrap It Up!

Technology is an essential component of modern education, particularly for online learners. A reliable computer and internet connection are prerequisites for effective participation in virtual classrooms, enabling seamless communication, collaboration, and access to academic resources. A good computer minimizes technical glitches, supports multitasking, and ensures compatibility with educational software, while a stable internet connection prevents disruptions during video conferences and file transfers. Together, these tools will enable you to fully engage in your studies, ensuring productivity and academic success. Additionally, staying updated with the latest technology helps protect against cybersecurity risks and ensures smooth access to educational platforms and tools.

Artificial intelligence (AI) transforms education by enhancing learning experiences and improving efficiency. AI-powered tools provide personalized learning by analyzing individual performance and offering tailored resources. AI also streamlines tasks like scheduling, organizing materials, and providing feedback, saving time, and boosting productivity.

Familiarity with AI tools like ChatGPT can help you prepare for exams, clarify complex concepts, and build confidence.

Embrace technology. It is vital for your personal and professional growth. Proficiency with emerging technologies provides a competitive edge in the job market, equipping you with valuable skills. Remember to love wisdom and keep seeking knowledge. By fostering an open mindset toward technology, you will not only stay relevant but also unlock pathways to advanced careers and meaningful contributions in a tech-driven world.

Chapter 15

PAUSE, PROCESS, PROGRESS

"Be still and know that I am God…" Psalm 46:10 (NIV)

I stared at my computer. It is the end-of-the-year performance evaluation for the employees. But instead of crunching numbers and rating questions with 1-5 on a Likert scale, I have three questions to answer. These are not verbatim from the evaluation tool, but the content goes something like:

"What went well?

"What can you improve?"

"What are your goals for the next school year?"

Only three questions, but they stopped me in my tracks to ponder and reflect on the past year and how I can move forward. I spent hours writing as I answered each question honestly and in detail.

As professors, we are encouraged to periodically reflect on our practice. As students, you will benefit from this practice, too. In the courses I teach, reflective essays are always included towards the end of the course. But what does reflective practice mean? Reflective practice is the process of thoughtfully analyzing your own experiences, actions, and decisions so that you can learn from them and improve your future behavior. It is a deliberate approach to self-examination. It can be structured or unstructured, but you must critically evaluate what you did, why you did it, and what the outcomes of your actions were. The main goal of reflective practice is to enhance your personal and professional development. Reflective practice is commonly used in various fields, such as education, healthcare, and management. This encourages continuous improvement and lifelong learning.

At work, we usually have mid-year and end-of-the-year performance evaluation. First, at the beginning of the year, we would set goals. Then at the mid-year meeting with my boss, we discussed the progress of those goals. By the end of the year, we present which goals were achieved and which ones were not. Then I will be asked what I think went well and what did not; what I learned during the process, and what I can improve on. This is an example of a reflective practice.

I also have personal goals outside of work. I have goals for my travel, education, finances, health, and other personal projects such as writing this book. I write them down at the beginning of the year. Throughout the year, around March, June, and October, I revisit these goals. I check off the ones I have accomplished. Then, I review what still needs to be done. Oftentimes, not all of those goals were met. I used to feel like a failure when I had some things on the list that were left unaccomplished. However, through the years, I learned to accept that it is OK! The Holy Spirit helped me to be at peace with what I could get done and not punish myself with guilt because of those unmet goals.

The Reflective Process

In Chapter 9, I have a section about self-reflection. There I discussed how self-reflection helps cultivate a healthy mindset. I also gave an example of how I processed some setbacks in the progress of writing this book. In the same way, you can start reflecting by writing down what went well with the goals that you have accomplished and taking note of what you can keep doing moving forward. It can be how you managed your time and stayed focused to reach those goals. Then, you can reflect on what did not go well. Ask yourself why you were able to meet some goals and not the others. Sometimes, things that did not go well were not because you were too lazy to accomplish those goals, but because circumstances beyond your control can happen. Some examples of things beyond your control are health emergencies, grief, job loss, or dire family situations. For biological women, you should also consider your menstrual cycle because there are days of the month when you are less energetic and may have terrible mood swings.[21] Be gentle with yourself during these days in your cycle. Know that nothing is wrong with you and this should only last for a few days. After reflecting on what went well, and what didn't, I then ask myself what I need to improve on.

Self-reflection on workouts that actually worked! For the past years, I kept struggling with getting my workout as part of my daily routine. I did not believe in gym membership because in my mind, it is ridiculous to pay for a gym membership when I can do workouts for free at home. Sure, I would be good at keeping at it for up to the first month of the year, January. I felt so proud of myself when I was able to complete a 30-day yoga just by following instructions from YouTube. But then when February rolls around, I would miss a day or two, and then it goes downhill from there. By March, I hardly get a workout done. Before I knew it, the year would come to an end and I would feel defeated in this area. This went on for many years. When I reflect, I would just say, I will try again next year!

In April 2023, right around the same time in the cycle of my previous failures, I seriously looked into what my problem was. I finally admitted that I needed help and I could not do this on my own. A regular gym membership (which by the way, I also tried many years ago), was also not for me because I could not do the routines on my own either. I prayed to the Lord to lead me to the right help that I needed. Somehow, right on cue, an advertisement of a free barre class at a nearby studio appeared on my Facebook feed. Long story short, I found out the reasons for my failures at working out. First, I do not do well without an instructor. I would stop when I feel tired. But with an instructor, and doing it in a studio with others, provided a healthy pressure to keep going even if I

21   Pelz, Mindy. *Fast Like a Girl: A Woman's Guide to Using the Healing Power of Fasting to Burn Fat, Boost Energy, and Balance Hormones.* Hay House, 2022.

am breathless, or get a little light-headed, or even when my muscles are hurting. I just need to keep going until the class ends.

Second, I can only do workouts first thing in the morning at 5:30. This took a while before I finally figured this out. There are many things that can happen during the day. If I schedule it around noon, I am already too hungry. If I eat before the workout, it makes me lethargic, and I hate burping while doing the sit-ups! Furthermore, things can happen during the day, such as an important meeting at work, or an event that my husband and I should go to. Lastly, I cannot do an after-dark class either because this is around the time when I'd make dinner. All the other times except for 5:30 AM does not work for me. Getting it done first thing in the morning sets the tone for the day. It paved the way for me to cultivate other healthy habits. In Chapter 5, I discussed my morning routines that I was able to establish after being consistent with my workout schedule.

Self-reflection on panic attacks. I have already shared in Chapter 1 how I overcame my panic attacks. Self-reflection is what helped me. In my academic journey, I often reflect after a course, or after a frustrating incident. There was a time when I was experiencing panic attacks whenever there was a deadline approaching. After a reflective process, I realized that the cause of my panic attacks was my expectation for myself to get straight A's. The solution that I discovered to mitigate my panic attacks was to, first, not procrastinate to give myself ample time to do a job worthy of an A. Second, I assured myself that a lower grade is fine. It truly is! A perfect GPA of 4.0 is not worth stressing and having panic attacks over! I had to remind myself what I always tell my students. What matters is the learning and experience gained through the process. This new mindset worked and my panic attacks disappeared. I enjoyed doing my assignments more by taking off the unnecessary pressure. Sure enough, I did not get a perfect 4.0 GPA, but I also did not have panic attacks. If you are experiencing panic attacks or other strong emotions, try to reflect on what causes them. Most of the time, by looking deeply within, you can find the answers you are looking for.

Reflect with Gratitude!

Reflective practice is a game-changer for a purpose-driven academic experience. Writing regularly and reflecting on your educational path helps you recognize the value and growth in your learning experience. Tracking your progress is encouraged so you can acknowledge how far you've come. This practice is self-motivating. You will recognize how your past actions contribute as the key driver to your progress.

The foremost focus of reflective practice should be gratitude. In Chapter 9, I also discussed how an attitude of gratitude cultivates a healthy mindset. Take time to list down things that you are grateful for. Write them in the present tense. When I was studying for my Ph.D., I had a list of things I was grateful for on a Post-it note. I put it up on my desktop. When I get discouraged, I repeat them to myself and tell my thoughts to dwell on positive things. Check out some of what I wrote in Chapter 9.

Don't Complain like the Israelites

The story of the Israelites in the Bible describes how they complained a lot while they traversed the desert on their way to the Promised Land. What would only take a few days to travel by foot, took them 40 years. Aside from the constant complaining, do you know what they kept repeating to themselves? "We will die in the wilderness!" And guess what happened? None of the original generation of Israelites, except for Joshua and Caleb, made it to the Promised Land. All of them died in the wilderness including their great leader Moses. Truly, death and life are in the power of the tongue (Proverbs 18:21)! So, watch out what comes out of your mouth. Be aware of words you repeat to yourself.

A habit of complaining can impede progress. Even new age beliefs attest that "negative vibes" and "negative mantra" bring no good influence in your life. And the Bible says the same thing! In everything, give thanks! Be grateful for every little thing. Find the good; find something to be thankful for even in your worst situation.

"Give thanks in all circumstances; for this is
God's will for you in Christ Jesus." 1 Thessalonians 5:18 (NIV)

Own Your Experience

Your academic journey is your own. You create memories of your experience. No matter how similar it may be for everyone else, yours is unique. Do not compare. You create the reality of your own experience based on your insights and perspectives. You have to declare that you are going to enjoy your academic journey. Every time you sit down to do your assignments, you are not doing it with a begrudging, complaining attitude. Rather, you are going to do it out of a heart full of joy.

You have to determine in your heart that with every assignment, you are going to learn. Learning is not limited to the content or knowledge that the process is teaching you. There will be times when an assignment looks worthless and it has no beneficial or redeeming factor worth your time. You have to look beyond the content to realize what you are learning and how it is shaping you as a person. Is it making you more patient? Is it teaching you how to deal with frustrations? Is it teaching you how to trust a process? Is it teaching you to just keep plodding along and keep moving forward no matter how tired you are? You have come this far. You can go even further by enjoying the learning process and embracing your unique timeline no matter how long it takes for you to get to the finish line.

Benefits of Reflective Practice

There are many benefits when you take time to stop, slow down, look back, reflect, and dump into paper everything that crosses your brain during the reflective process. Writing words on paper makes everything more tangible. When you can't quite put your hand into what the problem is, when you are confused, or when you cannot understand something, dump your thoughts into paper. Then when you have all the pieces in visible words, you can piece how they are connected and correlated, giving you the whole picture. This clarity brings:

Self-awareness. When you think critically about your actions, decisions, and experiences, it can lead to a better understanding of your strengths, weaknesses, and other areas for improvement. Remember my story about my panic attack episodes whenever I had a deadline to finish an assignment? When I took the time to critically examine the cause, I became self-aware that I had self-imposed expectations of holding a 4.0 GPA. I got rid of my panic attacks after letting go of the self-imposed 4.0 GPA goal.

Enhances continuous learning. When you reflect on past experiences, you can analyze what worked well and what didn't, leading to more effective problem-solving strategies and better decision-making in the future. You learn from every experience, both successes and failures. This mindset fosters adaptability and a willingness to embrace change. When you have consistent reflective practice in place, you can keep up with the changes of times. In turn, you will never grow stale and irrelevant. You remain fresh, relevant, and upgraded despite the changing times. What worked well five or ten years ago may no longer work today, and only through self-reflection will you be able to realize that.

Better communication and relationships. Reflective practice can lead to improved communication skills when you become more attuned to your own thoughts and emotions, as well as those of others. Better communication skills lead to better relationships. When you have good, peaceful relationships with others in your immediate circle like your spouse, children, family, friends, professors, and academic advisors, your academic journey will be positively impacted. Reflect on how you communicate. Imagine you are the other person. Are you communicating what you think, what you want, and what you feel clearly and appropriately?

Increases accountability, innovation, and creativity. You become more responsible and accountable for all your actions, the outcomes, or the consequences. When you do so, you become more cautious and careful when you take action because you know the impact it can have on yourself and others. This increased accountability leads to an innovative and creative outlook when identifying new ways to think and work for solutions to challenges.

Emotional intelligence. Reflective practice enhances your emotional intelligence when you understand and manage your emotions. Frustrations usually stem from places where you cannot name your emotions. Self-reflection can help explain your feelings. In one incident, I asked myself, "Why did it make me angry?" The answer to that question led to deeper truths about triggers, trauma, and a horrible childhood experience. After knowing about this, I can control my emotions better and start looking at recurring situations more objectively. Self-reflections can also bring healing to past wounds and trauma, increasing your emotional intelligence.

Let's Wrap It Up!

Reflective practice is the deliberate process of analyzing your experiences, actions, and decisions to learn from them and improve future behavior. It involves a critical evaluation of what was done, why it was done, and the outcomes achieved. By fostering self-awareness, reflective practice enables personal and professional growth. By evaluating successes and setbacks, you can identify patterns and understand factors that influence outcomes. Take time to reflect periodically to gain deeper insights in your learning experience.

THRIVE

Focus: Building a Strong Academic and Professional Future

> *"Trust in the Lord with all your heart and lean not on your own understanding; in all your ways submit to him, and he will make your paths straight." Proverbs 3:5-6 (NIV)*

What you are doing now is building your future. Every decision you make, every step you take, one day at a time, a little at a time, will become the picture of your tomorrow. Now is the time to plan and build forward while you are in the thick of your online classes. You want your degree to work for you and bring you a return of investment one day. You do not want a college degree that will be useless in your pursuits in life. Keep the big picture in mind and execute the details.

Your efforts today, build the GPA of your tomorrow. As an online student, every participation response that was posted, every discussion question answered, every quiz and exam taken, every assignment submitted, and all field experiences done, build your future. Each one is a building block towards that piece of paper called a diploma. Each one matters for that transcript of records that your future employer will look at.

While you are studying, you are building your resume. Whether you are going to apply for a job, or you are the employer, having your own resume will keep you on your toes about the experiences, skills, and other credentials one is looking for as a perfect job candidate. Education, job experiences, skills, and professional affiliations can be honed and fine-tuned while you are still studying. Do not wait until you graduate.

Even though you are getting a degree online, you should also build connections, establish relationships, and form networks of people who share the same interests as yours. While your family and friends are your number one support, your professional network will take you places in your career that your family and friends cannot. You can join social media groups for people in your related field of study. You need to look for online classmates who share the same interests, passion, and dreams as yours. Look for those who live close to your area and are willing to meet up for coffee or lunch. Look out for professors who can mentor you and help you develop professionally.

People, organizational, conflict management, problem-solving, writing, speaking, and technical skills are some of the outstanding professional skills that can enhance your resume once you graduate. Start developing and acquiring these even while you are still a learner. These skills are not specifically taught in your courses, but they are indispensable and can give you a competitive edge over other job candidates. If you are a business owner or an employer, having these skills and teaching them to your employees will encourage growth in your company and competence in your employees.

This last section makes you look forward and envision the big picture of your tomorrow. As you do so, there are practical steps you can take now that will prepare you for life after you get your degree. Finish what you started. Plan and build forward.

Chapter 16

GRADES WITH GRIT

> *"I can do all this through Christ which strengtheneth me."*
> *Philippians 4:13 (KJV)*

I came into the faculty room and wearily sank in my chair. I was exhausted after three hours of lecture and I was ready for a break. I took off my high-heeled shoes and raised my legs on the stool underneath my cubicle. I stretched my arms and closed my eyes, grateful for the respite.

"Ma'am," the dean's secretary's voice jolted me back to reality. My eyes fluttered open and saw his face hovering over me. "The dean wants to see you in her office. There's a student waiting for you." When I asked who it was, I knew it was an issue about the two points I deducted from her essay. This was an A+ student. What was she doing at the dean's office complaining about me? She had already talked to me and wanted the two points back. When I did not budge, she asked, *"Professor, is there any extra work I can do to rectify this situation?"*

At that point, I snapped at her. "Look, you can't always have a perfect score. It's only two points off because of misplaced punctuation and formatting. It's not a matter of failing or passing. You still have an A on your paper. You need to move on!" I waved my hand dismissively.

I thought she'd drop the issue. But apparently, this student was ready to escalate the situation to the dean's office and fight to get her two points back.

I quickly opened my laptop and pulled out the student's records. I marched into the dean's office, and a tear-stained face with two red puffy eyes turned to meet mine. I looked at my dean and we exchanged knowing looks. It's another case of an academically intelligent student with a low emotional quotient (EQ).[22]

The Two Extremes

I have had two types of extreme students over the years. The first one cares so much about their grade that a one-point deduction in any of their assignments triggers panic and anxiety. They can't sleep, they cry their eyes out, and they demand a clear explanation of why they did not get a perfect score. They ask if there is a way to get that one point back! For them, it is the end of the world when they don't get a perfect score!

On the other hand, another type of student doesn't care about their grade. As long as they are passing enough courses to remain in the program, they don't care if they get a D or C. They get an F from time to time, but as long as they are given the chance to retake the class and remain in the program, it is not a big deal. *"Professor, I would still pass the course even if I don't submit the remaining assignments, correct?"* For them, learning through the process is the least of their concern. They only want to get a degree, and if possible, just meet the minimum requirements.

As an online learner, I hope you are neither one of these. The first type who strives for perfection and excellence needs to learn that their identity is more than their grade. They have misunderstood the meaning of excellence, and they are not being realistic to expect that they will only get perfect scores on every assignment. On the other hand, the second type, who does not care at all about their grades, must realize that they are wasting money on their education if their transcript records reflect low to failing grades. At one point, their character will be judged based

---

22   Emotional Quotient (EQ), also known as emotional intelligence (EI), is the ability to understand, use, and manage one's own emotions in positive ways to relieve stress, communicate effectively, empathize with others, overcome challenges, and defuse conflict.

on their grades. Poor grades are not only equated to low intelligence, but they can also be a reflection of laziness, lack of skills, irresponsibility, and many other negative traits.

Both types of students are not ideal. They say that numbers don't lie, and neither do letters for each one have corresponding meanings: A for excellent, B for good, C for fair, D for poor, and F for fail. While there is a saying that C's get degrees, C's on your transcript sends a message to those who examine it. *This student is not good at communication. This student is poor in mathematics.* If your job is related to communication and you have C's in your communication courses while in college, this tells the hiring manager that you are not a good fit for the job. However, if you have a C in mathematics, and your job has nothing to do with math, then the employer might overlook that.

Why Grades Matter in Job Application

When you apply for a job, and the hiring team examines your application, they will look at your credentials first before they decide if they will call you for an interview. When they look at your academic transcript records and see a few C's or F's, you are not there to explain why. You cannot say, "Oh, that was the time I was going through a difficult season in life!" Unimpressed, these few C's and F's can turn them off, and you might not even get shortlisted for an interview. While there are many factors that a hiring team considers, low grades are perceived as red flags.

Would you trust a therapist with failing grades to guide you for better mental health? Would you want a surgeon with C's in their transcript to slice your heart open? Would you want a teacher with Fs and Cs to teach your child? I think you will prefer that professionals you deal with businesses with have excellent academic backgrounds. And when they don't, you don't have to see their transcript of records to know that. Their efficiency and effectiveness in the professional services they offer are evident in the work they produce.

As a current online student, you are in the perfect position to shape the record of grades in your future documents. Take each course seriously, even if it is the most boring one or just an elective that you need to take to meet the number of required credits. Choose electives, not based on how easy they are, but choose ones that hone your skills or add value to your field of interest. When I was taking my master's degree in communication, one of the electives I chose was about online teaching and learning. Little did I know that many years later, my job would be in online teaching. So, choose electives that would add value to your skills and interests and take those courses seriously.

If you have difficult courses (in my case, it was College Algebra 1), seek extra help. I told myself I would rather get a C and be done with it than an F, which means repeating it the second time around. I studied extra hard for longer hours. I sought tutorials from friends who were good at math. I thanked God I passed with a C+ and did not have to repeat the course. It was the lowest grade I ever had in all three degrees combined: bachelor's, master's, and Ph.D. But it was the hardest-earned grade of all! Needless to say, I never attempted to teach mathematics to anybody. However, do not warp your identity into a letter grade, a GPA, and a degree. There is so much more to a grade and academic achievements.

Albeit, a Grade Is Not All It Takes

An academic grade does not reflect the total person that you are. It does not show your kindness, compassion, sacrifice, and service. It does not say the struggles you went through, the difficult times you encountered, your defeats and your victories. It does not say that you are a single mom who is raising four kids alone and is working full-time while you are studying for that degree. A GPA does not capture how you were able to finish your assignments amidst screaming children, a dirty kitchen, a chaotic living room, and mountains of laundry to wash and fold.

Yes, your GPA is important, and by all means you need to keep it as high as possible for the sake of your future career. But know that once you have done your best, you can leave the rest to God; there is no need to stress out about not getting a perfect 4.0. Your GPA is but a tiny detail of who you are. You are a much bigger person than that. Thus, while building a great GPA for the future of your career, remember also to check the quality of life that you are making for yourself right now.

Academic Excellence through God's Eyes

In today's world, academic success is often seen as a measure of intelligence or potential. But for those who walk with God, striving for excellence in studies becomes something deeper. It is an act of worship: a calling to reflect God's glory through diligence and discipline.

Our efforts in school or any area of life aren't just for grades, trophies, or applause. They're for God. Studying, learning, and growing are ways we can honor Him. Our academic work should reflect gratitude for the opportunities He has given us. "Whatever you do, work at it with all your heart, as working for the Lord..." (Colossians 3:23, NIV). In God's eyes, wisdom isn't just academic. It's a precious treasure that builds character and sharpens discernment. It prepares us for life's challenges.

Diligence and excellence in academics hardly go unnoticed. Whether it's preparing for exams, writing essays, or solving math problems, our commitment can lead to open doors, leadership, and influence. "Do you see someone skilled in their work? They will serve before kings..." (Proverbs 22:29, NIV). So, as you study, don't be discouraged by stress or pressure. Let your studies be an act of faith. Excellence isn't just about being the best. It's about giving your best, for the One who gave His best for you.

Let's Wrap It Up!

Academic excellence is a worthy pursuit not simply for the grades. It builds your character and opens doors of opportunities. While some students may obsess over perfection and others may drift through with indifference, true success lies in a healthy, faith-driven approach. Do your best and trust God with the outcome. Philippians 4:13 (KJV) reminds us, "I can do all this through Christ which strengtheneth me." A GPA may matter in your career, but it will never define your worth. What matters most is your integrity, your growth, and how you honor God in the process. Build your grades not just for the transcript, but for the testimony it tells about your commitment, resilience, and purpose.

Chapter 17

OWN YOUR CALENDAR, OWN YOUR LIFE

> *"Let all things be done decently and in order."*
> *1 Corinthians 14:40 (NKJV)*

"Wow! I'm impressed at how engaged you are in our discussion forums!" I remarked to one of my online students. Dave responded to all 30+ students in our class when the minimum requirement for engaging posts was only eight.

"I hope you don't mind!" he messaged me privately. "I'm 81 years old and have nothing to do! I read all the posts and respond to everyone because I am bored." He ended the sentence with a series of laughing emojis. I was shocked. I looked at his records, and it was true. Then, I dialed his number and asked if we could chat for a bit. It's very rare when an older student piques my interest!

"Finally, studying is now my number one priority because my legs can't move around much!" he chuckled, and I was amused. "Can't do anything except read and write with these aging legs!" Dave had a golden sense of humor! He found it funny that he waited this long to get back to school. Then, he told me how he flunked college as a twenty-year-old, and had all these life adventures and mishaps. He served in the military, raised a family, and moved a lot. Even his retirement at 65 did not stop him as he and his wife traveled to different countries. However, his wife died just a few months earlier. Now, he needed something to occupy his mind and overcome his grief. That's when he thought of going back to school because it was his one and only unfinished business. "After I get this degree, I can truly say I've done it all. It would be my dream come true!"

To date, Dave was my oldest student ever. Although he joked that his slow, aging body made him prioritize his studies, it reminded me that people have different priorities based on their life's seasons.

Priorities Differ

Priorities for each one of us differ depending on our life's season. The majority of adults who decided to go back to school opted for online schooling because of priorities. Most online learners are in their prime, have a full-time career, are raising a family, managing relationships, taking care of aging parents, socializing with friends, and serving in their respective communities. There are also online learners in their late 50s, 60s, or 70s who are seasoned with rich life experiences. They want to get a college degree because it is the only thing they have always wanted but never had the chance to get. They have retired and now want a second career whether in teaching, social work, church ministry, or business.

You need to acknowledge that your priorities depend on where you are in life and the season you are going through. If you are in your 20s, you need to realize that your age is an advantage. There are some things in life that you can hold back until you get your college degree such as getting married or having kids. If you are in your prime and decide to go back to school whether to finish college, get a master's degree, or a Ph.D., be gentle with yourself, because pursuing a higher education degree in this season is daunting given the responsibilities you already have. If you have retired and just wanted to go back to school for some reason, please know that you are an inspiration to so many people. Truly, it is never too late to pursue your dreams. Being aware of the season you are in as you are pursuing your degree will help you align your priorities to what you value most.

Count the Cost

First of all, always remember that it was YOUR *choice* to pursue a degree. This is not forced on you, and it is not mandatory that you earn one. You chose to pursue a degree on your own volition. You should acknowledge that this education has a price and you have to pay the cost. In Chapter 1, I discussed the hidden price of education that we often do not think about when we first enroll. The cost of education is not just the amount you pay for tuition and other university fees, although that cost alone is a hefty amount. There are "hidden fees," because the cost of education also involves time, effort, sacrifice, emotional rides, relationship strains, and many more that are unseen behind the "I got this!" facade.

Now, the secret is to acknowledge these unknowns, expect the surprising challenges, and brace yourself for the waves that life throws at you while you are pursuing a degree. And this is where knowing and building your priorities can do the trick and make you stand firm when the waves start to rock your boat. Priorities of individuals may differ, but here are some things that we generally value and prioritize. It is up to you how you arrange them in sequence and assign the gravity of importance to each one.

God and Faith. Christians often quickly say that faith in God is the number one priority in their life. But how do we demonstrate and live it out? While you might say, "I go to church, pray every day, read the Bible, serve in committees, attend small groups, tithe, give offerings, and go on mission trips," others might pause and realize, "Hmmm, I can hardly pray and talk to God every day. And when was the last time I attended church?" At this point, I want to emphasize that balance is key.

I used to be deeply involved in church-related activities. Note that I said, *activities.* There is a difference between a *relationship* with God and *church activities.* You may be very active in church activities, which is good, but your intimate relationship with God can be suffering. Meanwhile, you can also be very intimate with God, but your season in life does not allow you to have time for church-related activities. Remember that the important priority is for you to have a deep, intimate relationship with God. The activity involvements come after that. You see, having an intimate relationship with God is not quantified by merely joining church activities. Cultivate a habit of praying every day, then add reading a passage or two from the Bible. Even if you spend only ten minutes doing this every day, it will make a huge difference in your spiritual and emotional life.

Sometimes I go on trips, like an academic conference, and my husband is not with me. In this time of temporary separation, we constantly communicate through texts or calls. If I don't receive a response from him the whole day, that will cause me to worry and vice versa. There was an incident when I visited the Philippines by myself. My sisters, their kids, and I went to the beach. Along the way, we lost internet connection and phone signal. For several days, we had no communication. He was worried but suspected as much, knowing how bad the internet connection could get in remote areas in the Philippines. After a few days, we got back to *civilization,* and it was a big relief to be able to communicate again.

Now, picture God and your relationship with Him. He is trying to constantly communicate with you, but how are you responding? Is a once-a-week *"I attended church"* enough to say that your relationship with Him is intimate? How do you think God feels when He is trying to connect with you through simple ways like sunsets, tweeting birds, or refreshing rain, and yet through the flurry of activities, you miss the *"call"* over and over again? Take time to stop and communicate with God every day. Make this your priority. No matter what season of life you are in, and no matter how packed your schedule is, take time for God. Stop. Pause. Reflect. Breathe a prayer.

"Cast all your anxiety on him because he cares for you." 1 Peter 5:7 (NIV)

Tell Him you are tired. Tell Him you need help with your assignments. Ask Him to give you JOY through the mundane assignments that don't make sense. Tell Him you don't understand the instructions. Tell Him you are so unmotivated to keep going and you have lost all inspiration. Then, remember to give thanks. Give thanks that in spite of your messy human condition, He is still good. His character never changes, and He is faithful that He will never leave nor forsake you in the middle of this. Thank Him for His grace because it is sufficient; even in your weakness,

He is strong. Thank Him that He who began a good work in you will bring it to completion. Thank Him that His plans for you are to prosper you and not to harm you, plans to give you hope and a future. Thank Him because He promised in His Word that He will fight for you and you need only to be still. Breathe prayers from the Word of God, and it will serve as your sustenance in this no-easy feat of getting a degree.

"My soul is weary with sorrow; strengthen me according to your word."
Psalm 119:28 (NIV)

Relationships. One of my mentors at the Ph.D. residency admonished us to make sure the faces we love will *still* be there on the day we graduate. It is sad that some sacrifice relationships in pursuit of life's ambitions. Many end up divorced faster than they can finish their program. Your relationships must be your priority above your studies. If you are married, your spouse comes first. Then, your children. The rest are secondary.

Do you have a needy friend who wants to go out for dinner on a Saturday night when you have an assignment due? You can say no to that friend. But what if it's your husband who asks you to go with him to his company's dinner on a Saturday night when one of your assignments is due? For you to be able to prioritize your relationship with your husband and attend that dinner with him, you need to sacrifice something else. Maybe your time for social media browsing, laundry, or house cleaning can be used to finish that assignment.

My husband and I watch college basketball games, and it became our shared interest. So, I made sure that schedule was plotted out in my weekly plan. Big assignments due on Wednesday nights must be done by Tuesday if there was a game that day. My friends asked me why I prioritize basketball games. I told them it wasn't the games, it's our time together that I protect. It is our opportunity to connect and make memories.

Many mothers pursuing online education would also attest to prioritizing their children without sacrificing their studies. They would never miss baseball games, piano recitals, school activities, parent-teacher conferences, and all the what-nots of children's schedules. Your presence and interests in your children's lives are important and you should never flinch on prioritizing them despite your own desire to get a degree. But how do you balance this out?

I have seen and heard of many creative ways mothers can multitask. There are mothers who listen to screen readers as their school materials are being read out loud while they are driving to their children's appointments. Some read or write while in the parking lot waiting for school dismissal. There are those who bring their laptops or iPads to type in one or two discussion posts while they are watching baseball practices. And there are mothers who wake up earlier or sleep later to do their schoolwork. If there is a will, there is a way!

Identify one or two of your most important human relationships and prioritize these above your academic pursuits. If you are not married and have no children, perhaps your most important relationship now is your parents, brothers, sisters, nieces, nephews, or a best friend. Whoever these top two relationships are, make sure that they will never feel abandoned or sideswept because you found your studies to be more important than them. Never miss their birthday celebrations, special occasions, Thanksgiving dinners, and Christmas parties just because you have to do an assignment. And when you go to these events, please do not take your laptop with you to do homework. Leave it behind. Don't even bring up your studies in your conversations with them. Be fully present and engaged about life outside the academe. Sometimes, you may need to sacrifice weekend trips or activities such as camping, fishing, boating, or hiking if it gets too much. However, remember to assure your loved ones that this is temporary. If you have healthy relationships, you will be surprised at how supportive friends and family can be.

Health. In Chapter 5, I discussed health in detail, so I wanted to emphasize here that your health should also be one of your top priorities. You will not be able to function well and reach your peak potential if you are not healthy. It is easier said than done, but it can be done! Focus on these three things that will contribute to your overall well-being: sleep, nutrition, and exercise. Taking care of these three things will make you healthier, and you will have more energy to do the tasks you need to perform, clarity of mind to make swift and efficient decisions, and a happy disposition to keep going.

Career and Jobs. Online learners ought to be praised and applauded for keeping a full-time job while pursuing a degree. It is very rare to hear of online learners who are full-time students with no other responsibilities and can fully focus on their studies (except 81-year-old Dave). Most online learners choose online programs because it is more flexible and convenient while pursuing a full-time career. Your job and any career-related activities may consume the majority of your time. Choose wisely which tasks you volunteer for. Now that you have added academic pursuit into the mix, you need to lay low a little bit in your job to balance it out.

My former boss once shared how she felt that she was left behind economically and professionally by her peers while she was pursuing her Ph.D. They were working hard, thus earning more, getting promoted, and accumulating wealth through properties and other material things they could afford. On the other hand, she was working minimum hours, earning less, and focusing on her studies. But she told herself, "This is only for five years! Then, I will get caught up with them!" Sure enough, after five years and with a Ph.D., she was promoted.

For now, you should try to work enough hours that would cover the important bills you have to pay such as mortgage, car, food, and education. Then, set aside other ambitions that add to your expenses such as accumulating material possessions, going on fancy vacations, or earning more to afford your dream house if this means you have to work more hours. It is not wrong to desire and work for these things, but remember that you also need time to study. These things will come to you at the right time, but for now, your focus and priority is your studies.

At work, it is exciting to volunteer as part of committees to plan events, serve in community extension services, and take on more shifts or responsibilities in exchange for more pay. But know that the time you need to do these things may take away your time for your other priorities such as your time with God, with your spouse, with your children, and with your studies.

If Possible, Avoid Life-Changing Circumstances

In Chapter 12, I discussed things you can control and things that you cannot control. While pursuing your college degree, *if possible*, avoid life-changing circumstances. There may be other people involved in deciding for these life-changing events, but try to resist these changes no matter how tempting they seem to be and wait until after you graduate.

Remember, the average time to finish a degree is four years or less. I'm sure it is hard to wait this long, but you need to focus on your studies if it is your priority.

What are some of these life-changing circumstances? Here are a few examples of exciting life changes: getting a job promotion, changing jobs, moving houses, getting married, having another baby, etc. These are all exciting and wonderful things, and they are all great blessings to have. But these can upset your routines and study schedules prolonging your academic journey. Practice delayed gratification. Think about how this applies to you as an online learner. Your priority now is your studies, and if other exciting things come your way, you can waive it for now. If these life-changing circumstances can wait, so be it.

What About Divorce?

I am saddened that some of my former classmates went through a divorce while in the middle of their academic journey. If the reason why you are seeking divorce is only because you are unbearably distressed and not because there was infidelity or violence, rethink and seek counseling instead. Usually, the stress brought on by academic studies can be so exhausting, impacting marriages.

Ask your spouse to bear it with you and wait until you are done with your studies before you decide whether divorce is the solution you want or not. The stress and strain from studying can be repaired through counseling. Ask your spouse to support you by being understanding of your chaotic schedule. Sometimes, a spouse doesn't know how to help. So, you can say that taking the kids to the park on a Saturday afternoon for three hours gives you time to do schoolwork. Tell your spouse that when you are stressed and anxious, the best way to help you is to get you a coffee, a snack, or give you a shoulder massage. Many times, the stress and changes that studying routines bring in the life of couples can cause so much distress that they think the solution is divorce. Remember, if you choose this route, you have to deal with court hearings for property division and child custody. This upset in your routines can impact your academic momentum even more.

However, if a divorce happens while you are studying, remember that you will be fine. You're not alone. There are many students who have gone through this, and they found the courage to keep moving forward. If you decide to take a break from taking courses, so you can focus on your healing, that is totally OK. Things happen, and your university will always be ready to welcome you back when your circumstances are better.

Stop, Start, and Continue

When deciding what and how to prioritize, sometimes you need to ponder what to stop, start, and continue doing. Putting a stop to something means you are giving it up so you can give time for other things that matter more. Then, there are things that you need to start doing. Remember the adage that you cannot expect a different result with the same method. If a method, a habit, or a routine did not work before in helping you accomplish your goals, then that means you should start trying something new. Lastly, identify what works for you and you can continue doing them. Let me share my stop, start, and continue habits when I was pursuing my Ph.D.

I *stopped* watching Korean drama series when I started pursuing my Ph.D. in January 2020. You know the unforgettable year that was 2020 when all of us were hit with the world renown pandemic called COVID-19. A lot of my friends would post on their social media about the Korean drama series they were watching. I used to be addicted to Korean drama series, too, so it was a hard decision to stop watching these shows, especially when my curiosity would torture me. I felt some pity for myself when I could not relate to their social media posts and the discussions going on about a particular drama series. I remember that I made a conscious decision to avoid, as much as possible, these drama series because I got hooked on them and they took a lot of my time away from more beneficial and productive things. I said as much as possible because there may be one or two Korean drama series that I was able to watch during my Ph.D.

I *started* writing and tracking my routines to help me with time management as I balanced life with a full-time career and graduate studies. When I was a teenager and was pursuing college, my schedule was in my head only. But now that I have multiple responsibilities and different roles, schedules can get mixed up. I tend to forget or miss something if it's not on my schedule.

I *continued* prioritizing what's important for me: God, relationships, career, and studies. I continued striving for excellence and progress, not perfection. I vowed to myself that I will not allow myself to be consumed with Ph.D work, and that I will have a life outside of it. If I have 20 hours a week to do my Ph.D. work, then I should finish everything within this schedule. So, I continued managing my time.

I believe that knowing my top priorities helped me accomplish more while living a balanced life. When all my priorities were in their proper places, I was surprised to find time for other non-essential things like attending concerts, going to museums, traveling, painting, reading books, watching movies, going out with friends, hiking, etc. Remember the illustration about the big jar with tennis balls, golf balls, marbles, sand, and coffee discussed in Chapter 12? I would attest that prioritizing the big things first before the smaller things allows you to make room for other fun things.

Organize, Automatize, Optimize

Each of us is given 24 hours a day. And yet, why is it that others seem to accomplish more? Now that you have a picture of the top five things you should prioritize: God, relationships, health, career, and studies, you need to strategize how to do things faster and more efficiently. You need to organize, automatize, and optimize things around you to give yourself more freedom and relief. It might take a while and it is difficult, frustrating, and hard at the beginning. But once you get started, the time you spend organizing, automatizing, and optimizing eventually pays off and gives you a much-needed break from time-consuming tasks.

Organize everything. So much time can be saved if you know where things are. For example, finding your wallet or keys is a waste of time. But if you have a habit of putting them in the same place every time you get home or are done using them, then you don't have to waste a few minutes just looking for them. For your academic journey, organize your files. I want you to know that knowing exactly where you saved that last version of the assignment you are finishing or where to retrieve that journal article you downloaded a couple of days ago will save you time, and prevent stress and frustrations.

Get into the habit of organizing things every day. Small habits such as picking up clothes on the floor, or straightening the couch pillows as you walk by help maintain order in the house. I find that as soon as I take the laundry out of the dryer, it is easier to fold them because they are not wrinkled yet. While I have food in the microwave for 2-4 minutes, I put some dishes in the washer. This clears the kitchen sink or counter a little bit. Find ways to organize as you go.

It is the same when you organize your coursework–create folders and subfolders. I have a Ph.D. folder saved in my drive; in it are subfolders named for each course. I numbered each course in the order I took them. For example, 1_RES-811 was the first course I finished followed by 2_ PSY802, the second one. In each course folder, I have other subfolders for files related to that course such as the syllabus, reading materials, assignments, etc.

I used to be so disorganized, and it took a long time for me to learn some organizational techniques. During my bachelor's and master's program, I just saved my files and did not organize them. Today, it's hard to hunt for a document I know I had but don't know where it's saved. You can start organizing what you have today and continue learning how to be more effective in it moving forward. With the availability of cloud storage today, it is a lot easier to organize files.

Automatize. Identify things you can automatize. Automatizing things means getting them done automatically. With available technologies, there are many things that you can automate. For example, a lot of bill payments can be automated online so you don't have to worry about paying them on time. You can subscribe for automated deliveries. You can do this for your essential needs. I have automatic delivery for our cleaning supplies, body wash, toiletries, etc. so that I never run out of them. You can adjust delivery schedules for once a week, to even as far as every six months. Automating deliveries of things you always need will allow you to have more time for other things. Identify them, plan carefully, and execute them efficiently.

Optimize. Technology can help you optimize your productivity so that you can have more time. Technology has been discussed in Chapter 14 in more detail. Sometimes, learning a new technology is daunting and can be frustrating with the fear of committing grave mistakes. You may consume a lot of time learning new technologies but once you learn how to use the latest developments in technology in your job, studies, or everyday life, things can get better and easier. Be curious and maximize the benefits of technology to optimize your productivity levels.

Work Ahead, Not Behind

Always work ahead, not behind. I already mentioned this in Chapter 12, where I discussed time management. If you are going on a trip for the weekend, finish your assignments ahead of time. If you are allowed to submit them early, do so. If not, try to connect to the internet real quick while on vacation, retrieve the assignments you finished ahead from your files, and submit them on time. In case you are going to a place without internet connection, let your professor know and ask if you can submit ahead of the deadline. Never get into the habit of submitting late and making your trips or other non-academic related circumstances to submit late. *"I'm sorry, we have a family vacation," "I'm sorry, my child has an out-of-town golf tournament," "I'm sorry, I have a doctor's appointment."* These are all lame excuses.

Decently and in Order

God's Word is full of admonition about getting things done decently and in order (1 Corinthians 14:40). We should approach life, work, worship, and studies with intentionality, excellence, and discipline, not chaos or carelessness. Our life and actions should reflect God's character, in which one of these traits is orderliness. "For God is not a God of disorder but of peace—as in all the congregations of the Lord's people," (1 Corinthians 14:33).

Put your priorities in your schedule. If it's not on schedule, it will never happen. Do you ever have friends you talk to and say you will go out for lunch but it never happens? Why? Because nobody set the schedule. Do you have a dream vacation, a dream project, or anything you said you would do but they remain as dreams? Why? Because they were never put on the schedule. If it is your priority, put it on the schedule.

"As you know, we count as blessed those who have persevered..."
James 5:11 (NIV)

Let's Wrap It Up!

Although your education is one of your top priorities now, remember to count the total cost. Not the monetary expenses only, but also the other facets of your life that must be adjusted. Take care of your spiritual life and remember God to strengthen your faith. Take care of your relationships, especially that of your spouse and children. You don't want to be marching on that graduation stage, getting your diploma, without your crew because you failed in relationships. Take care of your health. You must be healthy to function well and be at your best at all times. Take care of your career or job especially if this pays the bills. Take care of these priorities as you balance the wheel of life during your academic journey.

Always remember that this "schooling" is not forever. If you stick with it, you will be done soon. Keep that mindset and stay laser-focused on the academic tasks in front of you. Do each task one at a time. One word. One sentence. One paragraph at a time. If tiny steps a day are all you can muster to keep moving forward, then so be it. At least you are moving forward.

If possible, avoid life-changing circumstances while you are studying such as moving out of state or out of the country or changing jobs. Do not prioritize your schedule, rather schedule your priorities. Identify things or habits that you need to stop, start, or continue doing so that you can attain your goals and be successful. Be organized with your things, whether it be around your house or on your computer files. Automate things such as paying bills or automatic deliveries to take one job off your list. Optimize the use of technology to accomplish tasks faster. Organizing, automating, and optimizing may be very hard at the beginning but once you are set, things get easier. Lastly, always work ahead, not behind. Be a model of a true responsible and committed student.

Chapter 18

BUILD YOUR BRAND
BEFORE GRADUATION

"Let love and faithfulness never leave you; bind them around your neck, write them on the tablet of your heart. Then you will win favor and a good name in the sight of God and man." Proverbs 3:3-4 (NIV)

After I graduated from college, I was excited to hunt for my first real job. However, our college back then did nothing to prepare us for job hunting. Sure, they prepared us to *do* the job, but there is a gap between college graduation and a real job which is called *job application*. I did not know how to even start. This was early 2002 in the Philippines, and the technology then was nothing compared to what we have now. I studied the Lotus 123 computer program in high school and MS-DOS in college, but by the time I graduated, Microsoft Office was gaining traction and all the knowledge I learned about computers became obsolete.

Microsoft Office was more user-friendly but it was scary at the same time. Every keystroke was baffling for fear that work would disappear any time with one mistake. I did not have a personal computer and had no internet connection at home. These were luxuries we could not afford back then. YouTube tutorials were not a thing, and resources that teach you how to apply for a job were nonexistent.

So, I asked around for the how-tos and did what my equally clueless classmates suggested. I thought the more pages on a resume there were, the more impressive it would be. Since I studied full-time, I also did not have a job experience related to teaching. I racked my brain for all the seminars and training I attended while in college, and then my college degree. I thought a resume would start with my personal information such as name, address, phone number, height, weight, favorites, and hobbies. Thank goodness skin color or race is not a thing in the Philippines, or I would have included this, too. I chose the Comic Sans font and enlarged it to 14" to fill up the pages so that I could have at least two pages in my resume. They said that the more pages you have in your resume, the better! (Later when I became a college instructor, I learned that it only takes one page to impress a hiring manager.)

They told me my resume should stand out to be noticed among myriads of applications. Back then, we had to go to the company and leave our resume and letter of application at the security office. So, in my naivete, I printed multiple copies of my resume and cover letter on neon yellow bond paper. It literally stood out. My college friend and I went to different elementary schools, talked to security guards, and left a copy of our resume. Usually, people get a job through referrals of other people already working in a company, or in my case, school. So, if you do not know anyone, it is almost impossible to get a job out of pure chance.

I cringe every time I remember when I first started my quest for a job. I shudder when I recall what the first version of my resume looked like, my cover letter, and the bright neon-colored paper I used to print them. Looking back, I'm sure it was only by God's grace, not my bright neon-colored bond paper, that got me invitations for job interviews. Eventually, I chose the Christian school that offered a teaching position for fifth graders.

Many years later, I began working as a college instructor, and our team concocted a series of *English in the Workplace* courses. Eventually, we wrote textbooks for these courses. I wrote the second book in the series which was focused on writing. The first part of the book was about resume writing, and it felt very personal as I vowed to never let any of our graduates experience or do what I did when I first tried to apply for a job. Our graduates came back to us full of joy and appreciation telling stories of how they were able to exceed expectations because they were ready with everything the hiring manager asked from them.

Modern "Resumes"

Resume writing has evolved over the years. Today, a *one-page resume* highlights job experiences, education, skills, and other qualifications. Do not include personal information like I did, such as your home address, height, weight, hobbies, and favorites. Hiring managers will only glance at your resume quickly, and they should see the information they need right away. Nowadays, technology can be used to scan the thousands of resumes companies receive to produce a shortlist for hiring managers to review. Thus, it is important that you are mindful of the keywords you use. Match your wording to what the job advertisement is looking for so that scanners can select your resume. When you get a call for an interview, that is when you bring your *comprehensive resume*. This one has more detailed records of your accomplishments.

Now, a comprehensive resume depends on your age and job experience. The older you are, the more job experience, skills, training, certifications, networks, etc. you will have to list down. The rule of thumb in resume writing is to curate a specific resume for the job and company you are applying to. Weed out the irrelevant details that are not aligned to the objectives of the company or related to the job you are applying for. Remember that people's attention span is shorter nowadays and you want them to see the qualifications you have that would fit the job vacancy you are applying for.

For example, if you are applying for a teaching position, then include in your one-page resume everything that is relevant to teaching such as that time you volunteered to teach at a kid's church. Do not include your job experiences as a food server because this is not relevant to the position you are applying for. This irrelevant detail should go to your comprehensive resume as part of your job history.

Aside from a one-page resume and a comprehensive resume, another type of resume is a *video resume*. This can include footage demonstrating how you do your job. Some hiring managers will also check if you have a website, a LinkedIn profile, and social media handles such as Facebook, Instagram, and YouTube channels. Some jobs like photography require online portfolios of sample work. If you have an online presence, they will also read reviews or feedback about your professional service. I encourage you that while you are in school, start creating and building your credentials.

Career Experiences

Think about the college degree that you are pursuing right now. What kind of job or business do you see yourself getting involved in after you finish this degree? Now, redirect your thoughts to your job experiences that are relevant to this future job or business that you want to pursue. Are there any? For example, if you are pursuing a nursing degree, did you have any jobs in the past or present that are relevant to healthcare? If you are pursuing a teaching degree, did you have any jobs in the past or present that are relevant to education? Most job openings would say that they require at least two years of work experience in a related field.

If you don't have a work experience that is related to your degree, now is the perfect time to look for those job opportunities. Of course, I have mentioned earlier that if possible, avoid life-changing circumstances such as changing jobs because it will derail your routines. Adjusting to a new job is stressful and can put a lot on your plate. So, if changing jobs is not something you will consider, that is OK. But how do you work on a career experience that is related to your degree?

Volunteer Work

Volunteering at activities related to your career is remarkable. You can volunteer on a weekly, monthly, or yearly basis. My college degree is in elementary education and my first two years of job experience after college graduation was in elementary. Now, you may wonder how I became a college instructor–it was through volunteer work. I mentioned in the previous chapters that I joined an exchange program (IVEP) after working as an elementary teacher for two years. Here, I volunteered to help teachers in middle school and high school; this was how I started handling older students. When I was interviewed for that college teaching job, my interviewer concluded our interview and said, "OK, so you have experience handling older students. We will give you a call and let you know the results of this interview." With that, he shook my hand. After a few days, I got the call informing me I got the job!

I encouraged my college students in the Philippines to look for volunteer opportunities that are relevant to their degrees. The idea of volunteer work was pretty strange in our country because a lot of people had the mindset that one should get paid for any work they do. Somehow, my story rubbed off on several students. The next summer, four girls who were in a chemical engineering program volunteered at a chemical laboratory of a manufacturing plant. They worked as laboratory assistants. Most of the time they were assigned mundane tasks such as cleaning and putting away the laboratory equipment, or bringing them out. Some other days, they would just stand by, watch, and learn as others work in the laboratory. Their unpaid voluntary work went on for several weeks during their summer months.

Unsurprisingly, their work ethic and willingness to learn impressed their supervisors. Eventually, during their senior year in college, these students were offered paid internships when they needed to put in hours of field experience before they graduated. Some of them got a job offer right after graduating, and others easily got a nice letter of recommendation when they applied at a different company later on. Volunteer work may be unpaid, however, when done with pure intentions of the heart, it becomes a priceless experience.

Education

Your education can never be taken away from you. You can get fired from a job, get demoted, or change jobs altogether, but your education stays with you no matter where you go. Something in the Asian culture where I am from values education so much because it is most people's way out of poverty. My parents used to say that they had no earthly wealth to pass on to us and our education was the only gift they could give to us. I believe the same for you.

Congratulations on choosing to further your education and give yourself a lifetime gift. This is not an easy endeavor. It requires sacrifice, grit, determination, and persistence. As you go through the roller coaster ride in your academic journey, remember the big picture. One day, you are going to include in your resume a bachelor's, master's, or doctorate degree. Usually in a resume under the education section, only the tertiary education or degrees are listed down: bachelor's, master's, and doctorate degrees. Your K-12 education, although it is the foundation and most important part of your education, does not count in a resume.

Certifications and Licenses

Technically, getting certified or getting a license to perform a task is part of our education. However, do not write these under the education section. Rather, write another section where it says certification and/or licenses. Certifications or licenses in areas of health services, education, business, etc. can be perceived as an edge over other applicants because these show your love for lifelong learning and updated skills and knowledge. Everyone may be getting the same degree but your certifications or licenses are a big bonus.

I have taken a certification program for teaching English as a Second Language (ESL). It was a six-month program, and learners got "certified" after passing the final tests. This additional certification was my qualification to teach English even though my bachelor's degree was in Elementary Education, and I only took a few courses in English. I think this certification augmented my lack of English courses to teach in college. If an opportunity comes your way to take an exam to get certified or get a license, grab it. Right after college, I took a civil service exam. Passing the civil service exam gives one a license to work in government positions. Although I didn't need this license because I had no plans to work for the government, I grabbed the opportunity because my college classmates cajoled me into it. Today, I don't need the ESL and civil service certifications anymore because I live in the US now. But I put these in my resume for years, and they gave me an edge over other applicants in my younger years.

If you think that getting certified will serve you well down the road, try getting one as long as it does not become an additional burden for you. Nowadays, there are a lot of free or affordable certification courses or programs offered by top universities such as Harvard, Stanford, and

Yale that you can achieve for an additional laurel to your wreath. Google alone offers affordable certification programs in areas such as data analytics, project management, information technology, etc.

Transferable Skills

You may have a wonderful list of career experiences, amazing education, and impressive certifications and licenses, but transferable skills are what make you unique and valuable into an organization. Chapter 20 has detailed discussions about specific transferable skills that you should be aware of developing as you prepare for your career or business. These are what get the job done and done right. You may wonder why there are some people that get the job, but after six months in probationary status, they get dismissed. Or you may wonder why there are good employees and bad employees, great bosses and terrible ones. Transferable skills are not taught in college from a lecture podium. But your experiences in college, or should I say life in general, should have shaped your transferable skills.

If you have computer and technology skills, demonstrate what you can do. There is a lot that can be done with computers and technology, sobe specific. Say that you analyze data using SPSS,[23] design websites, invent applications for small businesses, etc. Don't just write that you have computer and technology skills.

Don't just say that you have leadership skills, or that you are in a leadership position. Rather, describe how you exude leadership skills when a situation arises. For example, instead of just saying that you were a president and founder of a small business, describe how your employees grew from 100 to 1000 during your time as a leader, or how you increased the company's profit from 1 million five years ago before you started to 900 million today. Read more about transferable skills in Chapter 20.

Professional Affiliations

Another thing you can highlight in your resume is your professional affiliations. If you do not have any professional affiliations yet, now is the time to join at least one. Start looking into clubs or organizations in

---

23   SPSS is a statistical software package widely used for data analysis, predictive modeling, and statistical analysis.

your university that are related to your profession. For example, there are business clubs, educators' organizations, health providers' networks, scientists' hubs, etc. If these organizations do not apply to you as an online student, try online groups on social media platforms. Through these online groups, you can gather information about events, conferences, and other opportunities for someone in your profession. You can also try to search LinkedIn for professional affiliations that you can be part of. Remember that you are a lifelong learner and being part of professional affiliations will help you develop professionally in your career long after you graduate.

Do Business Owners Need a Resume?

My business management students asked me this question, "Do WE need a resume, Ma'am? We are not going to apply for a job. As business owners, we will be the one to hire people." My response was, "Of course! How would you know you are hiring the right people if you don't know what to look for in their resume?" At first, I was offended that my business management students looked down on the course I was teaching. They did the activities half-heartedly thinking these were irrelevant for them.

Well, a few years later, some came back to me thanking me for making them do it because they either ended up applying for a job, or they used what I asked them to do in class to boost their business. So, yes. Even if you are currently holding a job and getting promotions in the same company that does not require you to create an updated resume, or you have your own business and you see no use of a resume, still try to make one. Sometimes creating a resume is a reflective process to see for yourself who you really are and what you have accomplished so far. In doing so, you can redirect your footsteps to get into the place you want to be in the future.

Let's Wrap It Up!

As a college student, now is the perfect time to prepare to write a resume. "Resumes" have changed over the years. Aside from the common one-page resume and comprehensive resume, there is also a video resume. Beyond these traditional resumes, there are social media platforms that employers check such as Facebook, Instagram, LinkedIn, and YouTube channels. Some jobs such as photography prefer a portfolio of previous creations, and these should be available in online platforms such as a professional website.

Whether it is a one-page resume, comprehensive resume, video resume, social media platforms, or online portfolio, the basic contents for these are the same. Work on your job or career experiences related to your degree, education, certifications or licenses, transferable skills, and professional affiliations.

"Each of you should use whatever gift you have received to serve others..."
I Peter 4:10 (NIV)

Chapter 19

NETWORK WITH INTENTION

> *"Walk with the wise and become wise, for a companion of fools suffers harm." Proverbs 13:20 (NIV)*

Over the years, I have encountered students who would lament that they could not find support from their family and friends. I have discussed making friends with other online learners in Chapter 8, and in Chapter 9 I discussed how finding support groups is part of cultivating a healthy mindset. The struggle of online learners to find relational support is especially true for first-generation students who are the first ones in their family pursuing higher education. They have no one to turn to in their immediate network for encouragement, support, advice, or help. Higher education can change your life if you seek to establish relationships with other professionals in your field of study. Surrounding yourself with other people who are in the same profession sharpens you, motivates you, and challenges you to develop and grow in your profession. Family and friends can be your core support (or not), but they cannot do what professional affiliations can do for you.

One of my classmates in my doctoral studies lamented that her family could not understand the nature of the hard work involved in getting a Ph.D. While talking to her, I realized that she was demanding from them the support and help that she could get from professional affiliations. For example, she was venting out to her spouse about how her methodologist critiqued the design of her study. Her husband stared at her blankly and nonchalantly said, "Uh-huh." She got mad at him for not showing an ounce of sympathy and understanding, nor having any input about the design of her study, nor acknowledging how her methodologist was being unreasonable. (Well, how would he know, right? *Design,* what?)

She then shared what was going on with her study's design, and then I gave input on what I thought she should do. She gave a sigh of relief and said, "I wish my husband could talk to me the way you talk to me." This lady was expecting and demanding encouragement, support, advice, and help from her immediate circle of friends and family. But they are not pursuing a Ph.D. like her. So, how can they give what they do not have? This is where building professional affiliations can be of great benefit to you and help you move forward.

Synergy Is Power

Synergy is getting energy from one another. I did not understand the power of synergy until I observed how it works within the company. One of the schools I used to work at was owned by a wealthy family. They own a conglomerate of companies such as water providers, car dealerships, banks, security agencies, insurance, phone services, etc. Guess who provides water around the campus? Where do employees get good car deals? Which bank did they tell employees to open an account in for their paycheck? Which agency provides security services for their properties? You get the point. They owned all these companies providing services to each other. The income flow stays within the conglomerate. The power and energy of each one is boosted from within. Each individual business adds value to one another by patronizing their own. This is how synergy works.

The principle in this business model of synergy can be applied in your life as an online student. You cannot get the energy you need to study by talking to people who never went to school as an adult. But with professional affiliations, you can crowdsource and ask for help with what's the best brand of personal computer to use for studying, how to do in-text citations, how to write academic papers, how to solve math problems, where to find resources for your science experiment, where to get referrals for interviews you needed for a course project, and so on. After you graduate, you can keep developing professionally. With your professional affiliations, you will learn about current issues, latest developments, most recent technological updates, training, and upcoming conferences. Some of what I learned about teaching when I was in college is no longer applicable to the students today. However, I am updated on current trends and developments in education because of my professional affiliations.

Through professional affiliations, you can see how you are doing compared to your peers. No, I don't mean that you should compare yourself to others in an envious or malicious way. But knowing how others are doing can motivate you and keep you on your toes. When I was taking my master's, I thought I was doing so great, getting high grades and a perfect GPA. I was feeling proud of myself, and thought I was really smart when I got an A at a particularly difficult course. Later, I found out that two of my classmates actually got an A+, which means a perfect score! Did I envy them? No, but it stopped me from gloating. This kept me humble, and I reminded myself that I still have a lot of room to grow and improve on.

You think life is hard and you are doing poorly? Ask around and you'll find there are people who are in a worse situation. You're not alone! That should fill you with gratitude knowing that your situation or performance in the class is not as bad as you think. Some students I talked to were hesitant to join professional affiliations and build connections with people there. "Doesn't that make us look like a gold digger?" Not if you think first what you can offer for others and not the other way around. Synergy is powerful but the relationship must be reciprocal. Make sure you are an added value to the group. You are joining professional affiliations to serve, and not just to be served.

Community Building

Your education is to help and serve communities. The idea of a community back then was the neighborhood where you live. Neighbors know each other, the children play outside together, and the church is somewhere in the center, surrounded by the homes. However, modern-day communities are very different. Neighbors hardly know each other anymore, children don't play outside with the neighbors' children, and the church somehow is losing its voice and significance in the community. When people say "community" today, it means the group of people they identify with. There is a Black community, Hispanic community, Asian community, gamers community, bikers community, etc. There are also communities for online learners.

However, many online learners struggle with the feeling of isolation. They are missing the fellowship one can find in a physical classroom setting. There are no classmates to connect with and build lifelong friendships that go beyond the courses and graduation. There is no laughter, no jokes, and no personal connection is established because the discussions in online classes are purely academic. After the course, students move on with their lives separately. But, for the most part, the reason for this feeling of isolation is having no sense of community and belongingness.

Identify professional affiliations that you can be part of. For example, with a college degree in education and as an English instructor in the Philippines, I needed to affiliate with an organization that supports English teachers. So I searched and joined the British Council as one of my professional affiliations. This organization focused on developing and supporting English teachers in the country. There were monthly events or meetings in their Manila office where English teachers could socialize through poetry reading, music, arts, literature reviews, etc. I found a community for English teachers through this professional affiliation. Time passed in my academic career and life goes on. I am no longer part of this organization today. However, I continue to seek affiliations related to my current interests.

Building Smaller Circles within Your Community

There were hundreds of English teachers in that organization. I met and talked to a lot of people every single meeting, but I connected more with only two of them. We communicated via text messages or calls to each other. We knew whether the other would attend or not. Sometimes, we would get coffee or lunch together before the meeting. Eventually, life went on and we went our separate ways. Although I have lost touch with these ladies, I am grateful for the time that we had together when I was in the early years of college teaching. God gave them to me as friends who walked with me in that season of my life.

So it is when you seek professional affiliations and join a community. There will be hundreds or even thousands of people there, but you need to put yourself out there and make at least one or two friends. Build relationships and establish connections that will hopefully lead to lifelong relationships. And even if it is not a lifelong relationship, that is OK. Just enjoy the season you are in and have close connections with people who are walking on the same journey as you do. For all we know, most people in life come and go and that is fine. Just like the bus ride I mentioned in Chapter 8.

Professional Affiliations vs. Community Building

Please do not get confused between professional affiliations and community building. When I was in college, the professional affiliations I joined were for educators (because my degree was in Education), for environmentalists (because I love outdoor activities like tree planting and neighborhood cleanup), and a Christian organization (where we meet once a week for Bible Studies). These are all professional affiliations. However, attending the events of professional affiliations is not enough. You should build your own community a.k.a. friendships within these professional affiliations.

Otherwise, you will not experience the real essence of community. Initiate conversations, make connections, get their contact information, and make your own social media groups for the little circles you are creating. Invite others to get coffee after the meeting, or maybe a group dinner. Then as your friendships grow, maybe you can attend events together, do community projects together, or once you trust them enough, invite them over to your house for special occasions like Thanksgiving dinner. This is how you build your own community within the professional affiliations.

Build or Join a Community of Online Students

In this modern time and in an online environment, things are different. It is easy and hard at the same time to build and join communities. It is easy because there is an availability of online communication platforms such as WhatsApp, FB Messenger, Instagram, etc. However, it is also hard because more people are distrustful of each other and are not interested to engage or initiate face-to-face meetings with other people from their online classes even though they live together in nearby areas.

My Master's in Development Communication was a fully online program. And just like most of what online learners feel nowadays, I felt isolated after the initial excitement died down. However, some of my online classmates started forming an online group outside of the course portal. We knew that after the course was over, we would never talk or connect to each other again. So, we needed an online venue where we could stay connected. Somebody posted a link to a Facebook group where a lot of us joined to stay connected.

That Facebook group became the magic sauce for our close-knit community and where I gained lifelong friendships to this day. After a while, even though we lived in different provinces, we decided to meet as a group in Manila, the capital city of the country. Some of my classmates drove 12 hours, some from other islands had to cross via ferry, and some even flew down to the city. We called it the grand reunion. It was such a success and it was the start of our great friendships. Then, we had regular end-of-semester meet-ups. Eventually, some people traveled together, or if they lived close to each other, they met up for coffee or lunch. We posted on our Facebook group some pictures, and people were happy to see that meet-ups were happening. This motivated them to initiate and find nearby connections, too.

Throughout the years, even after graduation, if one or two would visit a province, they would post on our Facebook group and ask if anyone was from the area and was interested to meet. One time I went to Baguio City and asked one of our classmates from there if she would be interested in meeting me for coffee. She came over and picked me up from my hotel and we hung out for coffee. Then there were times when people would post about job opportunities or freelancing stints. Our Facebook group also became a hub for us to look for resource persons such as editors, writers, speakers, etc. One of them invited me as a resource speaker to a group of government employees to talk about communication.

Many years after our graduation, before I moved to Arizona, my closest friends in this community gathered together for a nice dinner to say goodbye to me. One of our friends had already moved to Seattle, and so after a year in Arizona, when my husband and I traveled to Seattle, we met up with him and his little family. Many of us have moved out of the country and so the meetups became fewer. But just last year, we had a grand Zoom reunion. Looking at the friendships I found in this amazing community, I could not believe that we all started in an online class more than a decade ago and our friendship continued because of a Facebook group.

What You Can Do

As I said, times have changed and I've noticed that people are less friendly, and more resistant and cautious in meeting strangers. I cannot blame them because of the evil in our society where kidnapping, scamming, and many scary stories are becoming more rampant. However, the need for human connections and relationships has not changed. It takes bravery and enormous courage to approach people and make friends. Start by being engaged in the classroom. There are some people in your online class that you can connect more with than others. Continue to build rapport, familiarity, and trust.

In one of my Ph.D. online classes, one of my classmates has built this connection and familiarity as we were classmates in almost all of our courses. Unfortunately, our online platform was built in such a way that students cannot send private messages to one another. So, when we got to our last course before our dissertation, I responded to one of her posts and told her my sentiments about being glad that we went through this journey together, and that if she wanted to contact me, she could search for my Facebook account. She did, and since she lives close by, we went out for lunch and celebrated our significant milestone.

Sometimes in classroom introductions, people say where they are from. When you write your introduction, express that you are interested to meet up with anyone close by. Organize lunch or dinner in a public, safe place. Exercise extra precautions such as letting others among your friends and family know where you are going, who you are meeting, and what time you are expected to be back. Ask them to check on you if they don't hear from you after a certain time. Be discerning and make sure that you stay safe at all times.

Let's Wrap It Up!

It is important to foster meaningful connections in the professional sphere. There is value in networking within professional affiliations where synergy gives power for collaboration and advancement. Translate your education into opportunities for community building. A community of online learners provides space for you to share personal experiences and create a supportive network. This can enhance your educational journey and open doors to future professional opportunities.

Chapter 20

CREATED FOR GOOD WORKS

"For we are his workmanship, created in Christ Jesus unto good works, which God hath before ordained that we should walk in them,"
Ephesians 2:10 (KJV)

A degree is not enough to prepare you for the realities of the workplace once you become a professional. Through the years that I have taught the course, *English in the Workplace*, I have always emphasized to my students that on the day of your graduation, there will be thousands more, if not millions, around the world who are also graduating with the same degree. It is a tough competition. You need to have a competitive qualification more than your degree. This is where your transferable skills come in handy and make you shine bright. There are many skills that you can focus on; below are some for you to think about.

People Skills

Having people skills may not come easily and naturally for everyone. While others find it effortless to deal with all kinds of people, there are some of us who need to exert more effort. We need to be more mindful of how we come across to other people, and how we manage ourselves when we clash with those whose personalities are different from ours. An awareness of different personalities helps us be more accepting of other people's differences.

An example of two different personality types are introverts and extroverts. Introverts are perceived as silent and shy, oftentimes mistaken as snobbish or aloof. Extroverts are energetic and sociable, but oftentimes mistaken as loud and boisterous. Personalities are further differentiated based on the way people perceive things and make decisions or choices. If you train yourself to spot personality differences and learn how to appreciate each one in their unique abilities and gifts, then that is a good start to develop people skills. Develop a non-judgemental attitude. People are individually unique and different from you it does not mean that they are wrong and you are right. They are just different.

Aside from personalities, people in the workplace also have different roles and responsibilities. You are either in vertical or horizontal relationships with these people. Vertical relationships refer to those who are above or below you, or those who are your superiors or subordinates. Horizontal relationships are those who are on the same level as you; you call them coworkers, colleagues, or teammates.

Vertical Relationships. You are the person in the middle here. You have bosses or superiors to answer to, and you have people under your leadership that you have to guide and please as well. This is a hard job. You are sandwiched between two ranks and you have to satisfy both. Sometimes, your superior will make a decision and you are tasked to relay the message to your subordinates. If this is not good news, then your subordinates will get angry at you, not at your boss. What's that saying about shooting the messenger? Your job is to manage and pacify them, and then act as a mediator between the superiors and the subordinates to somehow come to a middle ground where everybody wins and is happy.

Horizontal Relationships. These are people who are on the same level of rank as you are. These are your coworkers, colleagues, or teammates; you will attend meetings with them, work on projects together, and try to outshine each other's work performances in a competitive spirit. Most of your social time at work will most likely be spent together. This is the group of people where you can find good friendships, establish cliques, and hang out or do things together outside of work. On the other hand, your worst enemy at work can also come from this group because you will find yourselves competing against each other, especially if both of you are vying for promotions.

The best advice I have in dealing with people is to always be kind. You can never go wrong with kindness. You will never be at fault at the end of the day when your superiors, subordinates, or colleagues see nothing but kindness, compassion, and sincerity from you. You will go a long way with this character and attitude towards other people.

Organizational Skills

Like people skills, being organized does not come naturally for some people while others appear to be born with it. Being organized and staying organized can be done if you create a system around you. If you are someone who is not fond of organizing, then getting started is hard. So, I suggest that you focus on one area of your life at a time. Once you develop this discipline, it will trickle down to other areas of your life. As an online learner, the best way to hone your organizational skills is the files on your phone and computer.

First, organize your schedules by categories such as academic, work, personal, and family. Some people do not like keeping a calendar but if you will only learn how to use a planner or digital calendar, you will be able to keep up with being organized. If you have multiple little children and a spouse, and they have a full schedule of their own such as sports practice and school events, being organized will keep you on top of your role as a parent and a spouse. Sometimes your spouse has something in their workplace that you are invited or expected to attend as well. Then, you have social life schedules as an individual, as a couple, or as a family. The visual reminders on your calendar will help you prepare for what is needed, where you need to be, and which to prioritize.

For your academic-related schedules, on your calendar, mark the due dates of all your tasks and assignments for the whole course or the whole semester. You know how slow or fast you are into doing a certain task or assignment. Plan a time in between those deadlines and work on your studies. Again, always work ahead and not behind. Give room for emergencies. Always plan on finishing tasks before the deadline. In case something happens, such as loss of internet connection, you will still have time to do it. If you wait until the deadline before you do your task and an emergency comes up, it will not give you enough time to do it. You will end up missing an assignment. Due dates are not the DO dates to submit your assignment.

Organize your workspaces, whether at home or in the workplace. Make a list of places that you need to organize. You can do one drawer a day in 15 minutes. Sometimes if you have many years' worth of treasure and trash stashed away in your closets, cabinets, and boxes, it can be overwhelming, so people tend to avoid organizing altogether. What you do is work on little sections a day. You can do 15 minutes, 30 minutes, or one day a week where you will do some organizing. It is not realistic to expect one day off when you can do all the organizing and cleaning; this will never come. What works is to do a little each day. For example, before you begin working on your assignment, organize that one desk drawer you have. As you wash dishes tonight, organize that one drawer where you have your utensils. Tomorrow, organize another one. Within two to three weeks, you will be done organizing your kitchen drawers. Then move on to one bedroom, an office, the living room, and so on.

Learn to let go of things that no longer serve you. It is OK to hold on to sentimental stuff, but sometimes, this is the reason why people become hoarders. Ask yourself, "If I pass away, would people still care about this particular thing I am holding on to? Would people care about my yearbooks, photo albums, books, magazines, clothes, paintings, mementos, and everything in my storage unit that I rent for $300 a month?"

In my early 20's, I was cleaning my bedroom full of stuff. I have mementos from childhood, tons of letters from church friends, and pen-pals from across the world. Yes, this was in the 90s, when snail mail existed and the only way to stay connected with friends was through letter writing. I have boxes from college such as notebooks, projects, illustration boards, and presentations written in Manila paper (yep, no PowerPoint yet). At this point, when I was doing this particular cleaning, I had pretty much moved on from my teenage and college life. I was in the new season of starting a career, and suddenly it hit me. Until when do I have to clean the dust from these old collections when they no longer serve me? Those seasons of my life in the past were fun, and I was trying to hold on to those dear memories, but a whole new life was before me and it was time to make new friends, do new adventures, and make new memories. I took all those boxes outside and set them on fire. Of course, I had a little ceremony with myself about saying goodbye to the letters I kept for so long, and all the other mementos.

My mom said, I might regret that action, but to this day, I never did. It was the most liberating and peaceful thing I ever did in the area of organization. My bedroom became more spacious, clear, and clean. In fact, I did not have to clean as much as I used to because there was less clutter. I took this principle of decluttering and cleaning a.k.a. getting rid of stuff since then. After a season has passed in my life, I declutter and keep only one or two mementos, some pictures, and then get rid of everything. Recently, after five years of marriage, I got rid of around five garbage bags full of documents and mementos from my immigration journey to being an American citizen, Ph.D., driving lessons, and onboarding process into a new job. I tell you, my office has never been more clean, and I felt like a heavy weight has been lifted from my shoulders. Being able to get rid of my stuff was a sign that I was ready to embrace a new season.

Being organized can be translated as a skill in the workplace. Accomplishing goals, managing projects, and leading teams require a certain level of organization. Being organized is worth it because it helps you save time by knowing where things are or what should happen next. Being organized will help you "get it together" during stressful times and when you are in a rush. If you will be given projects or must lead a team to accomplish a goal, your organizational skills will be very helpful. Throughout my career, I noted that the best leaders are people who are organized. They do what they say and hardly miss or forget things. They are on top of everything because they don't waste time looking for files on their computer, or recalling information when they need to accomplish a task. They know the exact logistics and processes involved to get things done.

As an online student, there are many ways for you to hone your organizational skills; you can start in the way you organize your files, office space, car, house, and multiple schedules. Organizing is a never-ending task, but once you set this motion into a regular habit, you will hardly notice the effort you put into it. Let organization be part of your habits and lifestyle.

Conflict Management Skills

Dealing with conflict was partly discussed in Chapter 10 as well. From your fighting children to having a misunderstanding with your boss, managing conflicts requires a certain level of skills. In fact, you may not be aware of it but you manage conflict every day. This can be between you and your children, you and your spouse, your children and your spouse, you and the reckless driver on the road, you and your closest coworker, or you and your current professor. Once you realize that a conflict is starting, try to practice a few things that will hone your conflict management skills.

Listen actively to what each party involved is saying. Sometimes, when you actively listen, their words have deeper meaning. Look for clues where they are driven by emotions or sentiments. Then, acknowledge those feelings but point them to the facts as well. Empathize with others by imagining what it's like to be in their shoes. Try to look at things from their perspective. Communicate your own perspective as well and seek for common ground. This common ground will be the stronghold so all parties are satisfied and can keep working together. Focus on solutions rather than dwell on what went wrong. Conflict management skill is demonstrated well when all parties involved end in a win-win situation.

Problem-Solving Skills

Problem-solving skills are similar to conflict management skills. However, problem-solving does not necessarily involve other people. As a student, try to solve problems on your own first before asking for help. Make sure you read everything and follow all instructions well to find the solutions. Sometimes there are students who are needy and ask for help in every small problem they face instead of discovering the solutions themselves. There are students who get angry at their professor and accuse them of being lazy when the professor sends them links to where they can find answers to their questions.

However, professors do this to train students to look for answers themselves instead of spoon-feeding them with the information they need. When we were young, my dad would point to encyclopedias, dictionaries, or books when we had questions about our assignments. If there is a word that we don't understand in the instruction that is blocking our comprehension on what to do, he would tell us to look at the dictionary. He doesn't explain to us what the word or the whole sentence means. When we asked for information, he wouldn't give the answers. Instead, he would tell us to read this chapter or this page from a book or from an encyclopedia, and we found the answers there.

In real life, people who find solutions for their problems instead of depending on other people for help possess an invaluable skill applicable not only in the workplace but also in their personal lives. Make sure that you teach yourself to solve problems and find creative and efficient ways to reach solutions. Nonetheless, knowing who to call and ask for help is also part of the problem-solving skills. For example, as an online learner, if you encounter a problem with your computer, you know that the professor is not the best person to ask. The best person to call is someone from the tech support team.

If you are having problems finding the most relevant resources for the topic on a paper you are writing about, you know that the best help is from a librarian, not your professor. This is the same principle that you apply in your everyday life when you know who to call when emergencies arise. You have the phone numbers of the best plumber, electrician, handyman, landscaper, veterinarian, doctor, etc. I have a friend who has a list of phone numbers for restaurants that have the best American, Thai, Chinese, Vietnamese, Mexican, and Italian menus. When she has guests and has no time to prepare meals, instead of stressing herself in planning and cooking, she just orders food for them. "If they don't taste good for the guests," she said, "then they can blame the restaurants, and I have saved my face from criticism." Part of problem-solving is knowing how and where to get the resources you need to get things done.

Writing Skills

In Chapter 10, we discussed writing skills as part of communication skills. This section further expands this topic as one of your transferable skills. As an online student, you have a tremendous opportunity to hone your writing skills. Right now, online education is heavy in writing requirements. Most, if not all of your course tasks and assignments, will be in the form of writing. As you move up the ladder of your professional success, more writing tasks such as emails, reports, and presentations will be required of you. Even with the prevalence of artificial intelligence (AI) tools that can produce written materials, you still need to hone that skill of thinking in such a way that your writing is humanized, relevant, and logically structured. People have the misconception that once they feed AI tools with commands, they will produce written materials that they can copy and paste. This is a wrong approach towards AI and is not ethical at all. Treat AI tools like a calculator. The calculator can produce numbers, but the thinking person behind it should know what buttons to punch. In the same way, AI can produce written materials, but the person behind it should know what commands to encode. Then, they should evaluate the suggested ideas from the written output to craft a humanized, relevant, truthful, and logically structured final output.

That said, you still need to learn the basics of writing rules such as grammar, capitalization, spelling, punctuation, cohesiveness, conciseness, and the logical flow of ideas. You need to learn how to create thesis statements, how to stay focused on the topic, and how to make sure the succeeding subtopics are aligned and relevant to your topic. Sometimes, AI tools use vocabulary words that sound robotic. One of my colleagues printed out samples of students' works and messages that were obviously AI-generated. In one of the messages, he asked the student a question. And the first word in the student's response was, "Absolutely!" The room burst with laughter. Furthermore, you should know the difference between facts and opinions because when you write in the workplace, you should support your opinions with other relevant research findings no matter how expert you may be. You should know how to format your paper in the citation style required, such as APA7, or how to cite other sources so you do not commit plagiarism.

Speaking Skills

Speaking skills were also discussed in Chapter 10 as part of communication skills. I included a discussion here of this again to emphasize its importance as one of the most sought-after transferable skills. Create videos of yourself speaking. Practice talking about a topic related to your career. Take a video of yourself and pretend you are speaking to a group of people. Posting it on your social media platforms increases the challenge level a notch. Going live on Facebook, Instagram, or YouTube is a notch even higher! I have some activities like this in the class that ask my students to post their video responses for others to see. This was not their favorite thing to do, however, it was good training for public speaking skills.

Podcasts, TikTok, and YouTube channels are all avenues for public speaking skills that can reach a global audience. You can muster yourself to speak in work meetings, in your children's parent-teacher conferences, or if you attend small groups in your church; you can practice your speaking skills by sharing to others your thoughts and opinions during discussions. Sometimes in group settings like this, shy people have the tendency to be quiet, but they are missing the opportunity to hone their speaking skills. Other ways you can practice your speaking skills are through business phone calls, video conferences, and face-to-face conversations with people. The more opportunities you grab to speak up, the more confident you will become as you learn how to process your thoughts while speaking, connect to your audience, modulate your voice, and express your ideas.

Technical Skills

In Chapter 14, I discussed technology. If you are open to learning new technologies as they evolve, your technical skills will always be at par with others. Learning how to utilize the features of Microsoft Office, different software, and artificial intelligence tools are just some of the technologies you can start with to hone your technical skills. Learning how to create products such as documents, fliers, posters, cards, etc. with Microsoft Office, Canva, or other software is an example of a technical skill that is valuable in the workplace. Technologies are ever-changing, ever-evolving, and developing, and there are so many versions and referrals by others of which is better. And all this chaos can be so overwhelming and confusing that it can easily trigger anxiety. So instead of trying to learn one, some people would freeze and stay put, refusing to budge by sticking to what already works for them. Remember the story of my student that I shared in Chapter 14 who refused to use Microsoft Word? Instead, she used pad paper to write her answers and took a photo of it to submit her work. Might I add that she stubbornly refused to learn the use of Microsoft Office despite the tutorials available. She kept submitting assignments her way. I had no choice but to fail her work until she eventually dropped the course and left the university. Sometimes, we get comfortable with one technology and we refuse to learn new ones. Are we like her in some ways?

Here are some tips. First, you need to keep in mind that you do not have to learn all of the overwhelming new technologies. Identify what you need, and what can be useful for you. Then, pick one that serves a purpose for you. Remember, technologies are here to serve you and not the other way around. Always dabble with new technologies and pick one to learn. If at some point you realize that it is not something useful for you, you can discard it and move on to the next one. Another example is creating short video clips. For some courses, creating short video clips is an optional task; thus, some students will avoid it if they can. But, creating videos is an opportunity for you to hone your skills in creativity, not only in speaking but also in video editing. It may take a lot of your time at first and cause you a lot of frustration, but the skill of creating videos would probably be one of the minimum requirements under technical skills that a hiring team would look for in near the future.

Created for Good Works

The point of presenting these transferable skills is for you to be aware that it is not just your degree that will pave the best career for you. As I mentioned before, there are thousands, if not millions of people graduating each year with the same degree. But, it is your other credentials and skills that will give you a competitive advantage. Nonetheless, I encourage you to develop yourself in a holistic manner. It is comforting to know that God created us for good works (Ephesians 2:10). Thus, we can be assured that the Holy Spirit will help us in our areas of weakness. God's grace is sufficient for us and in our weaknesses, He is strong! (2 Corinthians 12:9-10). Become a better person each day, fit for the plans and purposes God has for you.

Let's Wrap It Up!

Transferable skills add to your credentials in addition to your college degree. Skills in dealing with people or relationships, organizational, conflict management, problem-solving, communication skills especially in writing and speaking, as well as technical skills are all applicable in different areas of your life. Relational or people skills can be honed or practiced in your daily relationships such as with your children, spouse, family members, and friends as well as all people in your workplace.

Creating a system to organize and stay organized even in small areas of your life such as in your computer files or kitchen drawers is a good start to practice organizational skills. Conflicts are common but managing them well and arriving at solutions that make everyone comfortable is an invaluable talent. Problem-solving involves creative ways to solve a problem and this may include outsourcing or knowing who to call for help. Communication skills especially in writing and speaking can be cultivated on a daily basis. Technical skills can be sharpened when you embrace technologies that make you more efficient and effective in the tasks you do. Having awareness and intention to sharpen your transferable skills will set you apart from other graduates and launch you to success.

BEFORE THE BOOK

My Personal Journey

I was hoping to finish the revisions of this book before I attended a women's retreat in March 2025, but the busy life did not even allow me to start it. At the retreat, God spoke to me in so many ways. I know that He has been faithful at every season in my life, and He will remain faithful in the publication of this book. He impressed to me that my mess is His message and the tests in my life are testimonies of what He has done. I was thankful for that opportunity to spend time with the Lord and set my heart and intentions straight before opening this book's manuscript again and pouring my heart in its revisions.

After the retreat, I started the revision process again. With my beta reader's and editor's comments, I became convinced that the full narrative of my story should go to this last section. I wrestled with my thoughts as to whether I should include this narrative of my life or not. At the retreat, I told God that I didn't want this to be about me. Rereading what I wrote in the first draft made me cringe, and I wondered if I was being self-centered. After a lot of deletions or additions, I prayed and trusted that the Holy Spirit would cover my weaknesses. Some of these stories were already mentioned throughout the different chapters of this book. Should you decide to stop reading here because you are not interested in my personal narrative, that is fine. But if you continue to do so, I hope that my story blesses and inspires you in your personal walk with God.

My Big WHYs

In Chapter 2, I mentioned that I would discuss in detail my big *whys*. The big why for each of my degrees–college, master's, and doctorate, were different. The *why*, or driving force behind my college degree was my parents and my brother, Eli. Then, my master's degree was for myself, and job tenure. Finally, my doctoral degree was for my husband. My higher education spanned out for more than two decades so my *whys* were different based on life's seasons. But they fueled my tank and allowed me to plod along when the going got tough and surge all the way to the finish line. I failed two attempts in both a master's program and a doctorate program due to a lack of big *whys*. However, my background story, in all its accolades, glory, shame, and failures shaped and made me who I am today.

My Early Childhood

My big *why* when I was pursuing my college education stems from a deep family history of poverty. I am from Lumban, an old town founded in 1578 in the province of Laguna in the Philippines. It is still a third-class municipality to this day, and while I did not think we were poor while I was growing up, to Western standards, we were! And I only realized that when I came to America for the first time in 2004.

On the contrary, I *thought* we were quite rich. My dad had a stable job as a government employee and had a regular paycheck. My point of comparison was that of my playmates from the streets whose fathers were gambling, smoking, and drinking on street corners. They did random jobs such as fishing, carpentry, and worked in rice fields as laborers, and they had no steady income. On the other hand, my dad would dress nicely and go to work in an office. As a child, I fancied that working in an office was the grand dream. And then on weekends, my dad would serve as a pastor in the local church. Now, before you think that he had two paying jobs, let me clarify that this was a typical *village* church where most members had great needs of their own. Maybe he got a *love gift* from time to time, such as a kilo of freshly caught *tilapia*.

"Pastor, would you happen to have some change in your pocket? We just need some money to buy a kilo of rice. We have not eaten since last night and our young children are hungry," was the usual greeting of a member on their way out of church as my dad stood at the door to shake hands with everyone as they left. At other times, a member would hand him a *love gift* of freshly harvested cucumbers, pumpkins, or a kilo of freshly caught fish from our lake and say, "Thank you for your message!" His earnings from his professional job were for raising his children, but his free service to the church community was his passion.

My mom stayed home taking care of us five children. She resorted to many ways to earn additional income. She made stuff to sell such as vinegar from coconut water, *nata de coco,*[24] cookies, and macaroni chips. She raised pigs or chickens and sold them at the local market. She tried the embroidery business, but finally found her niche in sewing clothes and embroidered gowns, our town's unique cottage industry. My dad's regular income paid the monthly bills such as electricity, groceries, tuition fees, etc. while my mom's earnings went to miscellaneous expenses that came when raising five kids such as a school project that requires materials to buy.

Another reason I did not think we were poor was because our living conditions were a lot better compared to others in our area. My grandparents gave a partial lot from their own yard to my dad. Then, my parents skimped and saved to build a house on that lot. We moved there when I was seven but it was only the basic frame of a house–rough cement floors, hollow block walls, and a tin roof. There was no electricity, water line, or rooms. As years went by, my parents improved the house and built additional structures around it to create more space. Despite this, as a child, I really thought we were rich because some families around us lived in huts made of dried coconut leaves and bamboo, while we lived in a house made of tougher materials. During typhoon seasons, some houses would be flooded and submerged in water, and the strong winds would blow away parts of their walls or roofs; not ours though, because it was made of more sturdy materials that could withstand the strong winds and rains.

Aside from the difference in housing structures, I never remember a time we went hungry because there was nothing to eat, nor was there a time we were told to go to a neighbor and borrow money to buy a kilo of rice. Some friends I played with on the streets would come to our house and borrow money from my parents. Sometimes, instead of money, my

---

24   Coconut gel made from fermented coconut water. Once the fermentation process is done, the coconut gels are cut into small cubes, then boiled in water and sugar. It becomes a translucent, chewy dessert.

parents would give them a cup or two of rice grains. Yes, you read that right. The parents would tell their minor children to borrow money from neighbors to buy food. Social stratification is also evidenced by the food paired with rice. If it is with meat or fish, then you're well-to-do. If it's just vegetables in watery, salty, gingery broth, then you must be poor. There were those that scoured the trash bins of restaurants or fast food chains for food scraps. They would reboil these scraps in water, drain it, add salt or soy sauce, and survive on those. Looking back, I realized that I grew up surrounded by so much poverty. But none of my siblings and I experienced these, so relatively, we were indeed *rich!*

However, I remember that we were always on a tight budget. For example, my mom taught me to use only a small amount of oil when frying fish because that bottle of oil should last a whole month until my dad's next paycheck comes. Or a bar of detergent should be enough to wash a week of laundry. We had to wear the same "night clothes" for two weeks, changing into new clothes in the morning only and wearing it the whole day even though we got sweaty and smelly from playing outside. When we got sweaty during the day, we put a face towel on our backs underneath our shirts to save clothes, to save detergent, etc. because this helped save money before the next one came in to buy supplies. We had to turn off lights or appliances when not in use. We were not supposed to stand in front of an open refrigerator and think for a long time. We should know what we are getting and get it out quickly once we open the refrigerator door. According to my mom, that saved electricity and would lessen the electricity bill. If we did not use our household supplies and utilities sparingly, we would have to deal with nothing until the next paycheck.

Back then, if you were a government employee, your job was considered a stable one because once hired, you could never be fired. You may wonder why my dad got a job in the government when my playmates' fathers couldn't. Well, he got a college degree that came with many years of hard work.

My Dad's College Journey

Our town, Lumban, is well-known for its cottage industry called *Barong Tagalog*, a hand or machine-embroidered textiles that were later made into Philippine formal or traditional clothes. My grandma used to recount details of my dad doing hand embroidery in the morning or evening, between college classes, so he could have an allowance for his daily expenses.

To cover his tuition fees and other expenses, he would stop studying for a semester to save money by working at odd jobs in construction, rice fields, hog farms, etc. He would get odd scholarships here and there to augment other expenses. One organization that helped him through his college expenses was *World Vision*. In case you are wondering, there were no *student loans* as an option in the Philippines. We pay all education expenses in cash *even to this day*. He graduated in his mid-20s with a Bachelor's degree in Accounting. Then, he got a good job, got married, and started to raise a family. He vowed that his children would never go through what he did and he would support them through college.

How to Finish College According to My Parents and Grandparents

Growing up, my parents and paternal grandparents who lived nearby kept telling me over and over again to get a college degree. To do so, first I should avoid friendships with those of bad influences-especially those who get into smoking, drinking, and drugs. Unfortunately, our small town is infested with drugs that destroyed so many young lives to this day. Second, I should never get involved in a romantic relationship until after finishing my studies. Third, never get pregnant (teenage pregnancies were a prevalent problem in our community). These, according to their statistical observations from young people in our town, are the reasons why people could not get a college degree. In fairness to their perspectives, I had several classmates in high school that did get pregnant. My parents watched with eagle eyes whom I befriended in high school. And in a small town like ours, word gets around like a wildfire. Their ways of getting information are way more advanced than a modern webcam!

"Who was that guy that walked you halfway from school to our house?"

"Who were those girls you ate lunch with?"

"Do you know that the father of that girl you're socializing with at school is a drug addict? Do not ever go to their house!"

"You are 15 minutes late from coming home. I told you to go home straight from school! Where have you been?"

Initially, getting a college degree was not my dream or goal. I thought I would embroider, bake cookies, and write books. I was very introverted in high school; I did not have the desire to go out and explore the world. Then, I thought I would get married, be a stay-at-home mom, and live a quiet, happy life in our little hometown. Getting a college degree was my parents' and grandparents' dream for me. Imagine how different my life would have been if I had followed my initial dream.

Would Have Been of My Life

I went back to the Philippines in 2022 for a 10-day visit. As I was walking the street one day, I saw a woman embroidering by the front window of her house. I knew this woman– we used to play together on the streets when we were kids. Childhood memories flooded my mind, and my neurons started shooting many questions. Had she always stayed here in their house in our little town? We had been embroidering since sixth grade! Had she ever been out of our town, or out of the country? Did she know how big the world is? I felt a huge distance between us, and I was unsure if I should say hello. Then, I wondered, what made this gap between us so huge? I didn't know why it bothered me to see my old childhood friend, stuck in the same spot, still embroidering after so many years.

I mulled over these thoughts on my 24-hour flight back to Arizona. We used to play every day after school during elementary years. We giggled, laughed, fought, and explored the little corners of our neighborhood together with other kids. I guess what I tried to figure out was when our paths separated and how the chasm between us felt so huge that I could not even bring myself to say hello.

Where and when exactly did our paths separate? Ah, we went to different high schools. That must be it. But no, we would still bump into each other and chat from time to time. Was it in college? Was it when I started working? As I recalled each phase of my life and wondered when our last interaction was, I could not remember anything anymore after high school. Then, it dawned on me. If I did not have a college degree, I would be in the same spot, too, embroidering *barongs* by the sun's light filtering through our front windows.

- I would never have taught in an elementary school.

- I would never have joined an exchange program that brought me to America for the first time in 2004.

- I would never have traveled the world.

- I would never have pursued a Master's degree in Communication.

- I would never have taught in college.

- I would not be back in America now, married, with a Ph.D. in General Psychology, teaching online students at a Christian university in the Southwest.

After I got my college degree, my dreams for myself became bigger. Then, when I joined that exchange program in Pennsylvania two years after graduating from college, my vision for possibilities became endless, my worldview expanded, and the world became my oyster. My parents' and grandparents' dream for me to get a college degree reminded me of a similar passage in the Bible where the Lord says He has not only "dreams," but solid "plans" for us. And His plans are to prosper us, and not to harm us. To give us hope, and a future (Jeremiah 29:11, NIV)! If you think that is too hard to believe and very impossible to happen based on your current situation, then read Jeremiah 32:27 (NIV): "I am the LORD, the God of all mankind. Is anything too hard for me?" In whatever situation or circumstances you are in right now, is there anything too hard for the Lord that He cannot accomplish His plans and purposes for your life? Do you realize that it is only YOU and your faith (or stubbornness) that hinder the Lord's plans to prevail in your life?

My College Life

My big *whys* for pursuing a college degree were my parents and younger brother, Eli. My parents finally convinced me to go to college when I was sixteen fresh out of high school (I had an early start in first grade). Their reasoning that convinced me to go to college became my big why. I powered through my courses, enrolling the maximum number of courses allowed per semester which were 7-8 courses. For three summers, I was also enrolled full-time, finishing three courses each. Pursuing my college degree became a solitary journey because I did not graduate together with the classmates I started with. However, I formed a special group of college friends who were older than me in the last two years when I was preparing for field experiences. I was also elected as a president of a Science Club, and an auditor of a Christian Club which honed my leadership skills. There were many college activities, events, and opportunities. But, if they interfered with any of my classes, I would give them up. I was laser-focused on finishing in less than four years.

Three years and a half later, I was done with an education degree. I got an elementary teaching job with the condition that I would take (and pass) the board exam that year. Otherwise, my teaching contract for the next year would not be renewed. At that time in the Philippines, the board exam for teachers to get their license to teach was offered only once a year. While being a new teacher on my first real job, I was also reviewing for my licensure exam. I took and passed this exam in the middle of a school year and it guaranteed my contract renewal for the next school year. But behind this driven passion was a big *why* that was shaped by my parents' convincing power for me to go to college.

My brother, Eli, is three years younger than me. This means that we had one year to be together in college, just like in high school. To send one child to college was already a struggle on the family budget, and so this meant my parents would not be able to send two! There would be two options. My brother would wait until I graduate, or I would stop studying and look for a job to save for my next tuition. So, my parents told me to do the best I could to finish as soon as possible, find a job, and help them send my other siblings to college. It is common and culturally expected in the Philippines for the older siblings to help out their parents and send the rest of the younger siblings to college. My dad, though married already, also helped his parents send his younger sister to college.

As I mentioned before, in the Philippines, there was no such thing as student loans. Our economic status, that is, my dad having a full-time job, disqualified me from the meager scholarships usually offered only to those who really had nothing. Hence, to avoid either of the two possible scenarios, I enrolled the maximum number of courses allowed per semester which was 21 to 24 credit hours equivalent to 7-8 courses. And then, for three summers, instead of taking a break or working, I also enrolled in the maximum number of courses allowed which was nine credit hours or three courses that run for six weeks. I figured this would also save me from miscellaneous fees, transportation costs, etc. because my day was maximized by attending classes as much as I could. Miraculously, I never had a failing grade on a paper, quiz, or any graded work. To this day, I still hear my grandma saying, "You are setting an example to your younger siblings and cousins." I was the oldest child and grandchild on both sides of my family. The firstborn.

So the pressure and expectations became the fuel to my tank of intrinsic motivation. This burning fuel that my brother would not catch up with me in college, and that my younger siblings and cousins would see a good example, kept me going on nights I had to study for three or four major exams the following day. I had to plod through the torture of math courses, and had to bravely face my fears of public speaking with each classroom report. Ultimately, my vision of seeing the end in sight as I endured months of on-the-job training both in public and private schools was fired up by the thought that soon I would be done. Soon, I would get a job. Soon, I would have my own money and I could help out my parents in sending my other siblings to school.

First Attempt for a Master's Degree

As soon as I got my official transcript of records in college, I went out with two of my college friends to look for a job. Somehow, we ended up at a nearby university. It must have been the adrenaline and momentum of finishing a college degree that made us do the unthinkable. We enrolled in a master's program! To this day, I knew I did that because I succumbed to peer pressure. My only motivation at that point was to have an additional entry on my bare resume that I was pursuing a master's degree. I really did not think or pray about it. I just enrolled with a 500-peso downpayment—money I saved from my meager college allowance. The only way I could save money in college was to tighten the belt. There were days I would not eat lunch to save a few pesos and wait until I could get home to eat. So, I used some of my own savings to enroll in a master's program.

Imagine my parent's surprise when I came home and, instead of announcing that I found a job, I announced that I was starting school again in two weeks. To this day, I have not figured out yet if they were pleased or horrified at that announcement. I had just finished college a week ago, and schools were still in their month-long semester break! I assured them I would pay for it because I would find a job soon. And I did when I got an elementary teaching job as a fifth-grade adviser and teacher. I taught Science, English, and History to fifth graders. Then, I was also busy reviewing for my licensure exam, while also attending masteral classes on Saturdays. For two years, I powered through my masteral courses. That time, I found something new to dream about.

I wanted to become a school principal. Later on, I would have my own preschool. Then, I would expand it to an elementary school! So, I had about three courses left to finish before I had to take my comprehensive exam. Once I passed my comprehensive exam, I could start writing my thesis, get the proposal approved, collect data, then defend my research. Then, voila! I would have my master's degree by the time I was 23—three years after graduating from college.

Plans Disrupted: Exchange Program

I was on track with my goals and my dreams of getting a master's degree. But then, an opportunity came so big I could not let it pass. It was an opportunity to join an exchange program in America. We wouldn't get paid, but we would get a stipend and all expenses would be paid including flights, accommodations, medical, food, and transportation. I struggled as I weighed the pros and cons. First, it would disrupt my teaching career, my educational goals, my financial goals, and my love life. Yes, by that time, my parents finally gave their blessing for me to enter into a romantic relationship. But who gets a chance to go to America for free with a stipend for one whole year? This was a prestigious program and there were a lot of applicants. And out of so many applicants, I was chosen that year as one of the two participants from the Philippines!

If you wonder why I applied for that program if my heart wasn't into it, here's the background story. A friend of my dad told him that the application for this program was open and she believed, "your daughter is a perfect fit." She gave the application form to my dad and my dad told me to fill it out. I was half-hearted about it. But my dad said, "Just try and submit it. You don't even know if you are going to be accepted." So, just to please him, I did. Months later, I got called for an interview. Then, after another month, I was informed that I was accepted. Even at that point, I was not sure yet if I would be able to go to America because I still had to apply for a Philippine passport, and then apply for an American visa. All these processes took a long time and involved a lot of effort on my part as I had to travel to Manila repeatedly to get them done. When I finally did, I told the school principal that I would no longer renew my teaching contract for the next year.

Then, it was time to tell some of my friends and colleagues. Most of them discouraged me from going. They told me to stay and finish my master's degree first. Some said it was not wise to give up a good-paying teaching job for an opportunity that pays nothing. They planted questions and doubts in my mind such as America was too far. What would I do if this program was a hoax? How would I be able to survive for a year without pay? And what about my budding romantic relationship? What about my studies? I was on track to graduate in one more year, and I had such a great momentum going on.

Again, it was my parents and grandparents who encouraged me. They told me this was a once-in-a-lifetime opportunity that many other young people around us did not have. My grandfather even said, "You have nothing to worry about us. All of us are healthy and fine. I will make sure I'm still alive when you get back." So against all odds, I accepted the offer and flew away from the nest for the first time, all the way to the other side of the globe. To my American readers, I want to add this information that in the Philippines, it was normal for children to live with their parents as long as they wanted, to the point that most stay with their parents even after they get married and have their own children. That said, I was living with them all throughout college and in the first two years that I was working.

The International Visitor's Exchange Program (IVEP) by the Mennonite Central Committee (MCC) based in Akron, Pennsylvania was a big blessing to me. It became the pivotal point of my life when multicultural exposures, new adventures, and traveling to different states and Canada changed my perspective, expanded my worldview, and shifted my mindset. It was liberating, and I was never the same person after this magnificent experience. However, coming back home after a year, I felt like a piece of a puzzle that was reformed and reshaped while being gone, and I could no longer fit back into my old life.

I no longer wanted to become a principal and own a school one day. I had no more motivation to write my thesis and earn my master's degree. I felt like I had to be somewhere but I didn't know where. And I was very certain there was no future with the guy I was seeing before I left—we ended breaking up with finality. I felt disconnected, isolated, and a misfit in my own community.

ESL Teacher and College Teaching

After a month of getting back from the US, I found a new job at an international school for Korean students and I taught ESL or English as a Second Language. This one was far away from home, and I shared a house with other teachers. I liked the international atmosphere in the school, the presence of different nationalities, and the global competitiveness of the system. After sixteen months, my contract ended, and I decided to teach English in college. By then, I knew I was done teaching elementary and tutoring some high schoolers. But my love for teaching English grew, so I applied as a college instructor for English courses. During my interview, one of the questions they asked me was if I planned to finish my master's degree.

A master's degree was one of the requirements to get a job tenure in college teaching. As I mentioned before, job tenure or job security in the Philippines is important because it is an assurance that you cannot be fired easily. There are more college graduates than good jobs available, so job security is important and tenure is a protection that your boss will not fire you at his whim to favor somebody else. So to get a tenure, I went back to the university to finish my master's. Instead of going straight to finishing my masteral thesis, I enrolled in some English courses that I was interested in. At this point, I really had no focus or goal anymore. I could not envision going back to teaching at the elementary level and becoming a principal, nor did I want to have my own preschool anymore! I no longer wanted the big *whys* that used to motivate me!

I need to add that this masteral program was in a traditional setting. So, I needed to request my Dean not to give me Saturday classes to teach because I had to attend my masteral classes. Eventually, working five days a week, traveling eight hours in total to get to that university on Saturdays (due to heavy vehicular traffic), took a toll on me. I really had no motivation to finish the program in my master's. To make matters worse, after a year or two of dilly-dallying and dabbing in courses that were not aligned for the Educational Management curriculum, the personnel from the registrar's office informed me that five years had passed since I first enrolled in my master's program. This means that the courses I took in the first year had lapsed and I needed to repeat them. This was the straw that broke the camel's back. I decided that I would no longer spend thousands of more pesos to pay for graduate school. It was time to walk away.

Second Attempt for a Master's Degree

My big *why* for pursuing a Master's in Development Communication was to be at par with my colleagues who graduated from prestigious universities, get a job tenure, and teach communication courses. A lot of them had already earned their master's degrees and PhDs. I almost gave up getting a master's degree until my friend, Christie, asked me a multi-million-dollar question. "Do you see yourself pursuing another career other than teaching?" I thought long and hard. I was really enjoying teaching college. I could not go back to teaching elementary, a teaching position that does not require a master's degree to get a job tenure. Thus, I looked for another university and I found the program Master of Development Communication that best suited me and my goal to teach other communication courses other than English.

This master's program from the University of the Philippines was offered in an online format. In addition to the convenience that this online program offered, there was also a deeper reason for pursuing this degree. You see, I mentioned that I got my college degree from a local community college. Now that I had traveled the world–I mean, some parts of the United States and Canada to be exact–taught in an international school, and have become a college instructor, my educational background became one of my insecurities.

Most of my colleagues graduated from big universities in the Philippines, known as "The Big Four," somewhat akin to the "Ivy League" in America. When there were conversations in the faculty room and they shared mutual experiences and connections, I felt out of place. That time, I was also a faculty chair for the English faculty, and since all of them are graduates from the big universities, I felt so insecure. When they questioned my leadership or decisions for the team, I stood firm and assertive. Many thought I had a strong personality, but little did they know it was a facade, and my mask was covering all the insecurities and the imposter syndrome that bothered me. There were many times I cried to the Lord and asked Him why, of all faculty, my Dean trusted me and appointed me into this leadership position when I had no master's degree, and my college degree was from a far-flung, unknown community college from my province. God responded to my questions with this verse:

"Study to show yourself approved unto God, a workman that needeth not to be ashamed, rightly dividing the word of truth." (2 Timothy 2:15, KJV)

Where God leads, He also provides. Somehow, I saw an advertisement for this master's program at the University of the Philippines offered in an online format. I saw my chance to be a graduate of one of "The Big Four." This time, I prayed hard about it and listed down the reasons why I wanted to get a master's degree. I also listed the pros and cons once I immersed myself in my studies again. Of course, one of the cons was the time needed to study, but the winning pro was the mobility online studying allows. I didn't have to worry about opportunities that may have come my way within two to three years as I could move anywhere in the world and continue my studies. Remember that during my first attempt at a master's degree, everything went down the drain when an opportunity to go to America came, and leaving the country meant I could no longer attend the physical classes.

I breezed through my second attempt at a masteral program with joy and delight. My classmates and I formed a great bond. We met up in person in Manila, the central location for everybody else. We had end-of-semester meet-ups, Christmas parties, end-of-the-school year meet-ups, etc. When someone from abroad or another province was visiting Manila, we made an effort to meet this person face-to-face through dinner or coffee meet-ups in Manila. We had classmates from Laos, Singapore, Dubai, Italy, Brunei and far provinces in the Philippines. Whenever they said they would come to visit Manila, we arranged for in-person meet-ups. This was not initiated by the university. This was all our doing!

Some of our professors, on our graduation day, even remarked that our bond and friendship were worthy of a research paper about online learning. Some of my greatest friendships were formed in these meet-ups. I even traveled to other countries with some of the girls I met in this cohort. To this day, we still meet up whenever we can!

With clear big *whys*: To be at par with my colleagues who graduated from prestigious universities, get a job tenure, and teach communication courses; my second attempt to get a master's degree went smoothly and fast. This time I had joy and felt fulfilled, driven with passion and purpose. I finished it in two and a half years with high grades, made great connections with the university professors, and established great friendships with my online classmates.

First Attempt at a Doctoral Degree

I had such a positive experience from my online master's program that a year later after graduation, I decided that I was going to pursue my doctorate. You would think that by now, I should have learned my lesson that I should not start a graduate school program unless my big WHY is clear. Well, let me assure you that big *whys* may change while you are in the middle of finishing your program; this empties your fuel, making it not sufficient for the rest of your academic journey. This happened to me again, and I was like, "What the heck, Remilyn. You are a mess!" But would you agree that it is in our messes that God gives us our life's message? I think that the reason I am able to write this book is because I am not a perfect student and because of that, I can relate and empathize with those who are struggling and failing.

By this time, I decided that if college teaching is going to be my lifelong career, I better gear up and attain the highest education possible. So, I enrolled in the same university. I finished two years' worth of core classes, but this time, I was struggling again and I could not find joy and purpose in what I was doing. A few more classes and I would be ready to write my dissertation. However, I decided to quit.

Looking back to why I gave up, I think I did not even have a big WHY. I was just bored that the time I had used for studying during my master's was then vacant, and I had no better use of my time. So, why not take doctoral classes, right? Unfortunately, without a big WHY, I went the same path just like the way I did during my first failed attempt at a master's degree. It was a long story with complex details of everything not going right, with different areas of my life back then that added to the discouragement.

In the end, I decided that the pressure from my studies, my mental health, struggle to live a balanced life, and lack of joy were reasons enough to discontinue my studies. Unlike my master's degree, there were more assignments, and they were more complicated that they sucked a lot of my time and energy. Familiarity with my current professors, who were also my professors during my master's program, took away the novelty of learning something new. These and many other complex factors made me decide to stop.

Second Attempt at a Doctoral Degree

My very big WHY for my next attempt to get a doctorate was my dear husband. Two years later after quitting my first attempt at a doctorate degree, I got married and moved to the United States where my husband resided in Arizona. I got a teaching job at a university where there are tuition fee benefits for full-time employees. This time, I had a big WHY. You see, before I met my husband, I already felt that the Lord was leading me to go abroad. I applied for Ph.D. programs and scholarships in New Zealand. I got accepted into a program in a prestigious university, but the competition for the scholarship that would cover everything was pretty tough!

I was in the process of applying for scholarships, the last step before I could move and study in New Zealand, when I met my husband-to-be. That time, I got torn between choosing a Ph.D. program in New Zealand or encouraging a relationship with this guy. So, I prayed to the Lord that whichever was not His will for me, would He please remove and close that door. I got an email of rejection to all the scholarships I applied for and a marriage proposal all in the same month–November 2017.

A year later, in November 2018, we got married in Arizona. He knew of my dreams and was in full support of me pursuing a Ph.D. During the tumultuous season of dissertation writing, it was the thought that my husband would be disappointed if I stopped pursuing my Ph.D. that kept me going. Thus, I dedicated that whole dissertation to him! My big WHYs in pursuing a Ph.D. this time was to make my husband proud, be worthy of pursuing an academic career in the United States, and inspire my colleagues both in the university where I am currently teaching and in my previous job in the Philippines to also finish their PhDs. Getting a Ph.D. was like an unfinished business, a ghost that would forever haunt me if I did not get it done, so I knew I had to close this chapter and get it behind me before the next chapters of my life unfolded.

God Is a Redeeming God

Oh, how I hated myself for all my failures. But God is a redeeming God. You've probably had enough of reading my life's story on my big WHYs. But now you see how having the big WHYs in each of my degrees served as the fuel that drove me to the finish line. At both of my first attempts for my master's and PhDs that failed, my big WHY was not crystal clear. With the changing seasons, goals and *whys* may shift. In my own limited perspective, I can look at those as wasted years, wasted money, wasted efforts, and wasted time. But our God is a God of redemption, and He is redeeming even my failures so that He can use them for His glory.

God can restore to us the years that the locusts have eaten (Joel 2:25). The credits I earned on my first attempt at my master's degree were a good addition to my resume so I could get a college teaching job. Likewise, the credits I earned on my first attempt at a doctoral degree paved the way for me to teach communication courses in the Philippines, which then became my job experience that was included in my resume so I could apply to teach communication courses in the United States. Furthermore, without these bitter experiences of failed attempts at earning degrees, I would not have these stories to write about. I would think I am a perfect poster of an excellent student, and I would have no mercy and grace for my students who are struggling. Indeed, everything works out for good to those who love the Lord!

"And we know that all things work together
for the good of those who love God..."
Romans 8:28, (NIV).

KEEP IN TOUCH!

You're Not Alone—This Is Just the Beginning

Dear Reader,

Thank you so much for walking through these pages with me. Whether you read every word or simply found one line that resonated, I am honored that this book became part of your journey. You didn't just read a story or gather information but you took a step toward growth, hope, and wholeness.

Visualize. Choose. Overcome. Thrive.

And let me gently remind you that this is not the end.

Reading this book is only the beginning of something deeper. These words were never meant to stand alone. They are part of a larger conversation, one that includes *you*. The struggles you've faced, the questions you carry, the victories you're still chasing… they matter! And I want to keep walking alongside you.

If this message has touched something in your heart, I invite you to stay connected. I've created a space beyond these pages for readers just like you where we can continue the dialogue, support one another, and share tools for faith, focus, and perseverance.

Here's how we can stay in touch:

- **Visit my website** to explore resources, reflections, and updates tailored to your journey.

- **Join the mailing list** to receive encouragement, insights, and new opportunities.

- **Be part of the online book club,** where we go beyond the words, share stories, ask hard questions, and lift each other up.

- **Watch for upcoming events and offerings,** both virtual and in-person, that will help you stay grounded and growing.

This community is a space for connection, not perfection. You don't need to have it all figured out. You just need a willing heart and maybe a little room in your *inbox*. I believe in your journey. I believe in your ability to rise again, to hold tight to hope, and to walk in your purpose. And I believe that while your story is still being written, you never have to write it alone.

www.remilynmueller.com

***

A PRAYER FOR YOU

Let me pray for you before you close this book:

Dear God,

Thank You for the hands that held this book. Bless the hearts and the eyes that consumed the message across the pages. Holy Spirit, please speak and breathe life and healing in their lives as they move forward in their academic journey. Give them joy and peace in their hearts that surpasses human understanding. May every task and every assignment they do for their courses be done from a place of joy and abundance, not exhaustion and emptiness. Keep them physically and mentally strong. May their minds rest and stay in Your presence. Enlarge their territories and give them courage to obey You so that You can accomplish the plans and purposes that You have for them. Plans to prosper them, and not to harm them. Plans to give them hope, and a future. Remind them to be strong and courageous.

I pray that You will cover them and their loved ones with Your hedge of protection. Lead and guide them into right relationships, whether it be with their spouse, children, relatives, friends, and other acquaintances from their social circles. Protect their relationships, and surround them with new people who will help them in their academic journey, whether it be their professors, mentors, classmates, and others who will lead the way for them to become the professionals You want them to be.

I rebuke any works of the evil one that were meant to kill, steal, and destroy the dreams that You have placed in their hearts. You said in Your Word that no weapon formed against them will prosper. but that all things will work together for the good of those who love You. Truly, no eye has seen nor ear heard, neither has it entered into their hearts the things that You have prepared for them. I pray that You will strengthen them even though sometimes they cannot see beyond their present, messy, circumstances. Give them faith, strength, and love to keep holding on to You.

> "'The LORD bless you
> and keep you;
> The Lord make his face
> shine on you
> and be gracious to you;
> The LORD turn his face toward you
> and give you peace."
> *(Numbers 6: 24-26, NIV)*

This I pray, in the mighty name of Jesus Christ, our Lord and Savior… Amen.

-the end-

www.ingramcontent.com/pod-product-compliance
Lightning Source LLC
Chambersburg PA
CBHW021715120626
46545CB00004B/1574